Shifting Stacks

A Look at the Future of Theological Libraries in Celebration of Atla's 75th Anniversary

EDITED BY MATTHEW COLLINS, JAMES ESTES & MYKA KENNEDY STEPHENS

Atla Open Press
Chicago – 2020

Published by Atla Open Press, An Imprint of the American Theological Library Association (Atla), 300 South Wacker Drive, Suite 2100, Chicago, IL 60606-6701 USA

Published in the United States of America in 2020.

ISBN-13 978-1-949800-07-4 (PDF)

ISBN-13 978-1-949800-08-1 (EPUB)

ISBN-13 978-1-949800-09-8 (Paperback)

Cover Design: Simply Aesthetic Design

Table of Contents

Introduction

JAMES ESTES, LIBRARY OF CONGRESS, AND MYKA KENNEDY STEPHENS, LANCASTER THEOLOGICAL SEMINARY

R eligion and theology librarians, those who work in theological libraries, and those who are subject specialists within larger academic libraries are at the nexus of two rapidly changing fields. One is the field of librarianship, which has been experiencing fast-paced change since the advent of the internet. The other is the field of theological education, which is undergoing a metamorphosis of sorts as religious affiliation patterns shift globally. Within a US and Christian context, the decline of mainline Protestant churches has reached a point that seminary graduates are more likely to find a part-time ministry placement than a full-time pastoral appointment. In 2017, nearly one-third of seminary graduates were preparing for bivocational ministry, blending secular and ecclesiastical employment (Deasy 2018, 69). While these fields have been in a state of rapid change for quite some time, global society has experienced a newer and more abrupt change within the last year. The completion of this volume coincides with a global pandemic of SARS-CoV-2, a novel coronavirus that triggers the deadly COVID-19 disease. For the editors in a US context, it also coincides with a particularly acute period of civil unrest and racialized violence across the United States.

Within this context and in recognition of Atla's 75th anniversary, it seems appropriate not to look back at where religion and theology librarians have been and how we came to be at this milestone anniversary. Rather, we stand in the center of the whirling vortex of change around us and ask: What is happening here, at the intersection of the changing nature of librarianship and the changing nature of theological education? How do we continue to move forward with the forces of change in a way that strengthens and sustains this specialized field? Following generations of librarians before us, are there ways in which we can shift our stacks–reorient our thinking–to let go of outmoded and harmful tenets and make space for new wisdom and new discoveries?

A tremendous amount of change has occurred within the production life of this volume; more change than the editors could anticipate. The chapters included within this volume offer a glimpse into a vast web of emerging wisdom that continues to grow as religion and theology librarians grapple with social distancing, quarantines, and online modalities of librarianship. Consider it an invitation. *Shifting Stacks* invites ongoing consideration of a future that shifts and changes, seemingly with every collective breath. It seeks to facilitate conversation about these and other topics that may guide a reorientation of theological and religious studies librarianship that is adaptive and responsive to the changes in librarianship, theological education, and the broader global community.

Atla After 75 Years

In June 1947, a group of librarians and administrators met on the original campus of Louisville Presbyterian Theological Seminary at First and Broadway in downtown Louisville to discuss shared concerns about the role of libraries in theological education. They brought to fruition the creation of a professional association for theological librarians a year in the making. The conference, authorized by the American Association of Theological Schools (the predecessor body of the Association of Theological Schools in North America, or ATS), drafted a proposed constitution for the American Theological Library Association with the stated purpose "to study the distinctive problems of theological seminary libraries, to increase the professional competence of the membership, and to improve the quality of library service to theological education" ("Proposed Constitution" 1947, 75). With this gathering of seminary librarians was born the American Theological Library Association, or Atla (formally rebranded in early 2019).

Shifting Stacks was envisioned to commemorate the 75th anniversary of Atla's founding and sits in a lineage of earlier volumes: *The American Theological Library Association: Essays in Celebration of the First Fifty Years*, edited by M. Patrick Graham, Valerie R. Hotchkiss, and Kenneth E. Rowe–a festschrift of original essays published in 1996–and *A Broadening Conversation: Classic Readings in Theological*

Librarianship, edited by Melody Layton McMahon and David R. Stewart–a collection of noteworthy essays from the first sixty years of Atla's history, published in 2006. This present volume celebrates 75 years of history, but it is not a chronicle of Atla's deeds; rather, it examines the present situation of theological and religious studies librarianship and speaks to our future.

Theological librarianship sits at the intersection of theological education and librarianship, two dramatically changing areas of practice. Frank Yamada, executive director of the ATS, recently identified the current state of change in theological education noting the changing nature of diverse factors and their impact on theological education itself:

> Personal anecdotes aside, there are data and pieces of evidence that demonstrate that my personal stories are rooted in deeper trends that have been at work within theological schools over the past twenty to thirty years: mergers; enrollment and financial challenges; the need for new educational models (including the role of digital technologies); the changing nature of faculty work; increased attention on student formation; and the changing nature of student demographics. The forces behind these winds of change come from both broader trends in higher education and the changing landscape of religion in North America. (Yamada 2020, 24)

As these factors have shaped and changed theological education, librarians wrestle with overlapping concerns: What is the role of information literacy (or even basic research) in "student formation"? How does the increasing cost of databases and other online resources weigh on a library's often dwindling budget? With so much information available via the internet, do we need a library? How can libraries serve online courses or even fully online programs? Theological libraries are not immune to the broader issues that shape theological education, as any librarian can attest. These stressors are compounded by issues that shape academic librarianship at a higher level and include attention to new elements of library leadership and planning, including user experience (UX) design, open access (OA) and scholarly communications, social justice and critical librarianship, and the shared promise and challenge of emerging and constantly changing library technologies and systems.

With this in mind, the editorial board of Books@Atla Open Press issued a call for papers in early 2019. "What do theological librarians need to be ready for as we move forward in the 21st century?" we asked, inviting conversation on the changes underway in theological education, theological libraries, and the specialized field of religion and theology librarians. The topics we named were those that spoke to the current state of academic librarianship, such as collection development in a changing landscape, the impact of distance learning on higher education, the emergence of open access, and so on. The present volume is representative of the responses to this invitation and, as the contents demonstrate, *Shifting Stacks* provides a selection of valuable and insightful responses to our invitation. At the same time, there are voices conspicuously absent from this conversation–discussions which the editors sought to cultivate but were unable to. While *Shifting Stacks* gives attention to conversations that are shaping how religion and theology librarians will live into the future of our profession, not every important conversation that has a bearing on our future is addressed herein, particularly with regard to diversity, equity, and inclusion. The editors hoped for more conversations about the reality of changing individual and institutional member demographics in an organization that is historically White, Protestant, and American. Conversations about Black, Indigenous, and people of color (BIPOC) librarians in a profession historically marked and marred by racism; about lesbian, gay, bisexual, transgendered, and queer (LGBTQ) librarians serving in historically discriminatory institutions; or about the perspectives of non-Christian professionals in a predominantly Christian member body are too often muted. The editors sought more explicit and honest conversations about diversity, equity, and exclusion/inclusion, but none were forthcoming.

A Shifting Future

As manuscripts started to arrive at the end of 2019, news was breaking of a mysterious new coronavirus in the Wuhan area in central China. As infections spread and deaths were recorded, the World Health Organization declared a global health emergency in January 2020 and, in February, named the virus COVID-19. On March 13, as we were editing the chapters for this volume, the United States declared a national emergency. Within a month, it was becoming clear in the United States what was already evident elsewhere: 2020 was swiftly becoming the most important and tumultuous year in living history under the onslaught of a global pandemic.

As the virus spread, emergency rooms and intensive care units were overflowing, and businesses, stores, schools, and cultural institutions sent employees to work from home–or began to lay them off. Various regional governments began to issue lockdown mandates. As of this writing, COVID–19 has claimed more than 610,200 lives and made more than 14.7 million people sick (Taylor 2020). The anxiety and uncertainty of life amidst a pandemic dominates the minds of many, often exacerbated by inconsistent and anemic responses from local, regional, and national authorities. Many businesses that closed temporarily have shuttered completely. Countless communications from businesses, vendors, politicians, and community organizers sent to constituents as an attempt to ease fears often carried the same verbiage of compassion and commitment to the point of cliché. The ivory tower of academia was not immune. In March 2020, colleges and universities across the United States were forced to send students, faculty, and staff home, adapting face-to-face classes to online instruction, practically overnight. Bewildered and anxious students were at the mercy of equally bewildered and anxious faculty, most of them completely unprepared for a new crisis pedagogy. Staff and librarians struggled to help both. As the need for a socially distant pedagogy has not waned over the summer, administrators and faculties alike are attempting to discern the best course of action for the 2020–21 academic year.

Many of the ongoing concerns which seminary libraries have wrestled with and which are central to *Shifting Stacks* became, almost overnight, critical to the functioning of schools during a pandemic: the acquisition and use of electronic resources in teaching and research, the importance of open access resources for schools with fragile budgets, the challenges of teaching and serving an online educational environment. As administrations struggle to make decisions about phased reopening of operations in the 2020–21 academic year–often with minimal faculty or staff input, per reports on social media and elsewhere–libraries have to make significant adaptations in their operations and programming in order to serve an educational community reshaped overnight by an epidemiological crisis. Many of the topics that this volume sought to address were no longer merely theoretical issues; they became hot spots in the new educational landscape. The editors believe that this volume offers meaningful and important contributions to this conversation, while also acknowledging that the urgency of the novel coronavirus pandemic and its impact on higher education and academic libraries calls for material far more reflective of the new educational landscape.

The tumult of 2020 was not limited to the COVID-19 pandemic. The ongoing pandemic of racism reached a crisis peak during this time as well. On May 25, 2020, an unarmed and incapacitated Black man named George Floyd was killed by police in Minneapolis, Minnesota. The video recording of the event, one in a long series of unjust and senseless African American deaths, sparked a period of civil unrest and protests not seen in recent memory. The Black Lives Matter movement and its allies cried for social justice while protesters took to the streets with the message, "I can't breathe," and calls for reform and reparations. Police brutality and systemic institutional racism, which once hovered in our periphery, now commanded our attention. Universities, alongside academic and library organizations, issued statements condemning racism. Racial and ethnic groups within professional organizations, like the Black Caucus of the American Library Association, led the charge, which entire professional associations followed, like the Association of

College and Research Libraries and the American Library Association. A few grassroots statements emerged as well, from librarians moved to show solidarity and speak out against systemic racism that is pervasive in our institutions and collections. These statements embody our starting point as a profession and the need for focused efforts to dismantle White privilege and address systemic racism in both libraries and academia.

This is the cultural and social context of this volume's publication. Thus, the major concerns around diversity, equity, and inclusion identified earlier as a significant lacuna in this volume's contents are even more telling. We, as White editors, are fully aware of and lament the lack of dedicated BIPOC perspectives in this volume. We are also aware of the disproportionately large contribution from male voices in this volume compared to the percentages of men and women in Atla's membership (Bailey-Hainer 2017). Although we actively sought additional contributions from BIPOC and women librarians, the fact that we were unable to gather these contributions are a worrying sign of larger systemic issues and inequities within our profession.

A Call to Conversation

The major markers of 2020 (as of this writing)–pandemic and civil unrest–suggest more urgent realities of academic librarianship that demand further attention. Conversations in both librarianship and theological education are developing as we grapple with the current moment, emergent questions, and new discoveries. In addition to the topics covered in this volume, we invite readers to consider the following: What are the conversations that need to take place in our specialized industry, either as new areas of research or critical inquiry, particularly given the ongoing changes in higher education and libraries? How will we follow our conversations, statements, and reports with the hard work of response, reform, and action? We cannot deny that the nature of our profession as librarians in theological education and supporting religious studies degree programs is shifting dramatically and rapidly. It is not unreasonable to expect that additional shifts will continue as we live into an uncertain future. While the threat of COVID-19 has changed the ways in which we interact with one another and carry out the work of librarianship, the persistence of racism demands that we look carefully at the systems in which we participate and seek justice, reparation, and true reconciliation.

This volume's call for papers, issued in early 2019, mentioned several emerging topics that are not touched upon in the contributions we received. Upon review, there are several topics on that list that are highly relevant to the present reality.

There is a tremendous need for more study and reflection on these and other issues to strengthen theological and religious studies librarianship for an uncertain future filled with change. Therefore, we take this opportunity to re-issue a call for conversation on these topics, particularly issues linked to identity, online modalities, library assessment, and systemic racism and prejudice.

Before we can move our field forward, it is important that we define, or perhaps redefine, our identity. The first group of librarians who gathered in 1947 to create the organization that became Atla called themselves theological librarians. The adjective "theological" strictly means relating to the study of theology, though our field now includes librarians in a broader range of contexts. The chapters in this volume refer to theological librarians and theological librarianship, as well as religion and theology librarians and theological and religious studies librarianship. For some in our association, identity as a theological librarian relates to a sense of call and/or recognition of library work as ministry by an ecclesial body (Keck 1996; Stephens 2007). For others, it does not. Atla launched a new brand identity with the tagline, "collectors & connectors in religion and theology" as a reflection of the organization's vision and strategic plan (Bartholomew 2019). While the legal name did not change, the new brand effectively and strategically minimized three terms that members had long bore as defining marks, appropriately for some and inappropriately for others: American, theological, and library. Following this shift in association identity, it may also be time to reconsider the terms theological librarian and theological librarianship when referring to the identity of Atla members and their work.

As libraries are linked to their institutions of learning, we must consider the impact of distance learning and online classes. Given that many librarians are now supporting students in online classes, we are experiencing *en masse* the challenges and opportunities of this modality of teaching and learning. It is undeniable that, as library services have also shifted to an online environment, our understanding of information literacy and information literacy instruction is also changing. It has become even more vital to stay abreast of current research in religion, theology, theological education, and academic librarianship. How does one do this on top of working full days, perhaps from home with distractions of family and pets, in an understaffed and underfunded institutional setting?

Library assessment practices may also need to be reevaluated as pandemic reality becomes a new normal. Suddenly print circulation statistics cannot accurately reflect the inherent value and importance of a library's collection to its patrons. Electronic resources are becoming more crucial for online courses and students sheltering-in-place away from campus, but the statistical standards for evaluating use of these resources are changing, too, as COUNTER4 makes way for COUNTER5. Furthermore, the rapid pace of change and uncertainties that accompany life in a pandemic make long-range planning difficult. How do librarians assess collections and services when these span physical and virtual spaces? How can libraries and librarians plan for inevitable yet unknown change? Are there strategies our libraries and institutions may employ that will cultivate an adaptive culture of responsiveness, rather than a reactive culture of chaos or, worse still, a stagnant culture that becomes quickly outmoded and irrelevant?

The demography of librarians in our association is shifting, slowly, away from predominately White, Protestant, heterosexual men and women. It is essential that we recognize this and act on it. How might Atla encourage membership growth among underrepresented populations? What systemic issues hinder our progress for a more equitable distribution of power and privilege in our field? A necessary starting point may be to center diversity, equity, and inclusion so that empowering BIPOC, LGBTQ, and religious minority voices becomes a focus of our conferences and publications, rather than token contributions from the margins. There is much work that needs to be done within our libraries, our institutions, and within Atla to simply begin addressing systemic racism and prejudice, much less dismantle it entirely.

These issues and questions are essential to consider if our profession is to move forward into the future in a strong and sustainable way. There are many avenues available for those who feel inspired to speak or write about any of these issues or other emergent topics that are not named here. The Atla journal, *Theological Librarianship,* is one venue for articles and essays. Those seeking an opportunity to speak might consider submitting a session proposal for a future Atla Annual. These topics would also make an excellent book proposal for a scholarly edition by Books@Atla Open Press. Please consider this an open invitation to submit your ideas, reflections, research, and more to one of these venues.

The Conversations in this Volume

What do theological librarians need to be ready for as we move forward in the twenty-first century? What is happening at the intersection of these two trajectories: the changing nature of theological education and the changing nature of theological librarianship? These are the questions the editors posed to the Atla community, and we received diverse responses from across the field. The conversations that we have included in this volume are indicative of the issues and concerns relevant to the future of religion and theology libraries–although they may have more urgency now than when they were written, given the impact of COVID-19 on finances and operations of religion and theology libraries and their home institutions. As librarianship itself is a continuously changing field of practice, the editors offer the essays herein as important participants in an ongoing conversation–but not as the final word or only voice that matters. Rather, they are an invitation to further inquiry and continued dialogue.

For many Atla members, theological librarianship is fundamentally connected to the formational goals and purpose of theological education itself. Christopher A. Rogers, in "A Holistic Model of Engagement," offers a reflection on theological education in terms of transformational theological literacy: how does theological education formatively engage with a seminary student's vocational commitment? How can that seminarian engage critically and authentically with their religious tradition throughout their faith formation? Throughout his reflection, Rogers examines the pedagogical purpose of theological education and reflects on how the seminary library can be a meaningful and deliberative partner in this process of formation.

One of the most important developments in scholarly communications is the emergence of open access as a means of disseminating and accessing new research outside the economic barriers posed by traditional scholarly publishing. In "Foundations for an Open Access Policy," Andrew Keck identifies precedents in the distribution of religious literature in early Jewish and Christian history and addresses the scholarly imperative of promoting knowledge as foundational supports for a theological library's support for open access. He provides strategies for identifying challenges and engaging with key players to provide support for the development of an institutional repository and transforming the theological library from an information consumer to a knowledge producer.

While librarianship continuously develops and deploys technological innovations, some theology librarians may feel unprepared to follow these trajectories. In "Embracing the Future of Digital Libraries within Theological Libraries," Paul A. Tippey considers important advances in digital library collections, and suggests technical, economic, legal, and social barriers that must be addressed as theological libraries redefine themselves in light of these advances. Tippey discusses how these barriers have been shaped and considers factors that must be addressed so that theological libraries are better equipped to move intentionally into an increasingly digital future.

Digital humanities–broadly seen as the application of computational tools and methods to the humanities disciplines–allows for new ways of analyzing and interpreting texts and corpora. In "Topic Modeling as a Tool for Resource Discovery," Shawn Goodwin and Evan Kuehn introduce us to topic modelling as one important digital humanities tool for examining texts and identifying research-relevant patterns. They walk readers through a project that analyzes a body of texts from migration studies and public theology, in order to better understand the process and use of topic modeling for theological research in emerging fields of study.

Collection development is not a new discipline, but librarians continuously refine its practice and develop new approaches to growing a library collection. In "Current Trends in Religious Studies and Theology Collection Development," Megan E. Welsh and Alexander Luis Odicino closely examine both traditional and emerging practices through a study of professional literature and survey response data. Their survey of collection development librarians at seminaries and other research libraries reveals a wide array of collection development activities and anxieties, in light of patron needs and institutional context, emerging digital resources, and the challenge of declining budgets, ultimately supporting the need for flexible and adaptive collection development strategies.

Librarian conversations about the future of libraries and collections are generally oriented toward growth and transformation, or at least survival in precarious times. In "Giving Libraries Their Due," Stephen D. Crocco addresses a much different aspect of the future of theological libraries and their collections. We cannot ignore the fact that several theological schools are closing or merging, oftentimes transitioning their libraries into a new existence either as a collection embedded in another library or dismantled and disbursed. Using the metaphor of organ donation and transplant and drawing on his experience with embedding the Andover Newton Theological School's library collections into Yale Divinity School, Crocco makes a case for a considered and ethical process during these types of library transitions.

Atla is historically situated in North America, but it has long-established relationships with colleagues across the globe. In "Atla Down Under," Kerrie Stevens and Siong Ng share the history of the Australian and New Zealand Theological Library Association (ANZTLA) and the collegial relationship that that association and its members have formed with Atla and Atla members. While this global perspective from Oceania cannot speak for perspectives from other parts of the world, this chapter does highlight the growing opportunities for collaboration and the exchange of ideas across nations and cultures. Stevens and Ng show that the experiences of religion and theology librarians in the United States and Canada are shared by our counterparts in Australia and New Zealand. There is a global future for our field. When we embrace resource sharing and cooperation on a global scale, there will be no limit to what we are able to innovate among our libraries.

This volume concludes with a reflective and inspiring chapter by Carisse Mickey Berryhill. Known among the most recent members of our guild as the professor of LIS 568 LE: Theological Librarianship at the University of Illinois Urbana-Champaign's iSchool, Berryhill reflects on her coming of age in the field and how our profession may weather the inevitable changes ahead. Drawing on biblical wisdom and the history of transition and change faced by our predecessors in this field, and directing her words toward the clear anxieties of 2020, Berryhill encourages us to stay connected with one another and find strength in our commitments to stewardship, service, and wisdom.

We humbly offer this collection of wisdom as an overture to a much larger and deeper conversation about the future of our field. Amidst a global pandemic, faced with unfathomable uncertainty, there is opportunity. It is a chance to look more deeply into ourselves, more deeply into our work as religion and theology librarians, more deeply into the systems we construct, support, and participate in, and to find openings for embracing change. This kind of conversation is essential not just to survive, but for theology and religious studies librarianship to thrive as the twenty-first century progresses.

Works Cited

Bailey-Hainer, Brenda. 2017. "Atla Members by the Numbers." *Atla Blog*, February 14, 2017. *www.atla.com/blog/atla-members-by-the-numbers/*.

Bartholomew, Jennifer. 2019. "The Next Chapter: Realizing the Atla Vision." *Atla Blog*, March 11, 2019. *www.atla.com/blog/the-next-chapter-realizing-the-atla-vision/*.

Deasy, Jo Ann. 2018. "Shifting Vocational Identity in Theological Education: Insights from the ATS Student Questionnaires." *Theological Education* 52, no. 1: 63–78. *www.ats.edu/uploads/resources/publications-presentations/theological-education/2018-TE-/2018-TE–52–1/63–78%20Deasy.pdf*.

Keck, Andrew J. 1996. "Information or Divine Access: Theological Librarianship Within the Context of a Ministry." In *The American Theological Library Association: Essays in Celebration of the First Fifty Years,* edited by M. Patrick Graham, Valerie R. Hotchkiss, and Kenneth E. Rowe, 172–82. Evanston, IL: American Theological Library Association. *books.atla.com/atlapress/catalog/book/6*.

"Proposed Constitution." *Summary of Proceedings: Conference of Theological Librarians.* 1947. Louisville, KY: Louisville Presbyterian Seminary, June 23–24, 1947: 75–6.

Stephens, Myka Kennedy. 2007. "The Ordained Theological Librarian: A Cost Benefit Analysis." In *Summary of Proceedings: Sixty-First Annual Conference of the American Theological Library Association,* edited by Sara Corkery, 142–52. Chicago: American Theological Library Association.

Taylor, Derrick Bryson. 2020. "A Timeline of the Coronavirus Pandemic." *New York Times,* August 6, 2020. *www.nytimes.com/article/coronavirus-timeline.html.*

Yamada, Frank. 2020. "Living and Teaching When Change is the New Normal: Trends in Theological Education and the Impact on Teaching and Learning." *The Wabash Center Journal on Teaching* 1, no. 1 (January): 23–36. *doi.org/10.31046/wabashcenter.v1i1.1580.*

CHAPTER 1

A Holistic Model of Engagement

Theological Literacy, Education, and Libraries

CHRISTOPHER A. ROGERS, MUNDELEIN SEMINARY/UNIVERSITY OF SAINT MARY OF THE LAKE

St. Augustine's often-analyzed dictum in Book XIII of his *Confessions—pondus meum amor meus*, generally translated as "my weight is my love"–conveys a concept of love not as a weight or burden to be borne, but as one's own weight or selfhood by which they are directed, moved, and transformed. Understanding this formulation requires delving into the field of ancient theoretical science, the pre-Newtonian conception of gravity in particular. Augustine illustrates his familiarity with classical physics in this passage in referencing the precept that each of the elements that comprised the cosmos–air, fire, water, and earth–had a proper realm to which it belonged, a natural place toward which "a body by its weight tends to move." Fire tends to move upwards, a stone downwards, Augustine noted. "They are acted upon by their respective densities, they seek their own place" (*Confessions* 13.9.10).[1]

Augustine's interest in adopting these prevailing cosmological tenets was not so much to identify or explicate the physical processes of causation in the material world as it was to apply these principles in a teleological manner to an explanation of the movement of objects through space in terms of their end (*telos*), design, or purpose they served. The significance of weight for a body rested not in its upward or downward movement but in its following the direction that was intended for it–its own place or the place proper to it. Thus Augustine writes, "Weight is like a force within each thing that seems to make it strain toward its proper place" (*Expositions of the Psalms* 29.2.10). Moreover, objects which are not in their intended position become "restless. Once they are in their ordered position, they are at rest." Achieving this rest Augustine therefore equated with order or stability. Rest is defined as a place or destination, the end for which a body's movement was intended. Unrest, on the other hand, was indicative of an absence of proper order, the unrealized natural movement of a body to its final and purposed end (*Confessions* 13.9.10).

Augustine's ultimate concern, of course, was not the movement of inert physical bodies across space but the disposition of one's own self or soul, and his genius lay in his ability to apply these theoretical constructs of physics to the human person in relation to God. "My weight is my love," he wrote in concluding this passage from the *Confessions*. "Wherever I am carried, my love is carrying me" (13.9.10). Love was the agent, principle, or force for Augustine that ordered and moved human beings to their proper and natural place of rest. He expresses in a similar vein that "the weight of bodies is, as it were, their love, whether carried downwards by gravity or upwards by their lightness. For the body is carried by its weight wherever it is carried, just as the soul is carried by its love" (*De civitate Dei* 11.28). In Augustine's theological anthropology, all beings hold a fierce desire for their own proper place and order, and for human beings that place and order is determined by their love. Love in this sense is a principle of movement: we move physically or mentally in the direction we tend–toward the beloved, the object(s) we love or desire. Augustine cautioned at length of the dangers of being displaced or misdirected by improper, inordinate, and disordered loves, "our love of lower things" or impermanent and fleeting goods. Human life was a pilgrimage toward one's ultimate destination, which for Augustine could only be life with God. "You gathered me together from the state of disintegration in which I had been fruitlessly divided," he exclaimed. "I turned from unity in you to be lost in multiplicity" (*Confessions* 2.1.1). Only God's love and love of God could provide the wholeness, direction, place of rest, and order one sought and was intended to receive. To love in this manner is to move toward God who awaits us. "You stir [us] to take pleasure in praising you," Augustine proclaimed in the first paragraph of his *Confessions*, "because you have made us for yourself, and our heart is restless until it rests in you" (1.1).

Augustine and Theological Literacy

How does one move from a consideration of Augustinian anthropology to an exploration of methods and approaches to literacy in theological education in the twenty-first century? And what critical roles should theological libraries and librarians take in contributing toward and advocating these pedagogical principles and practices? The objective of this chapter is to illustrate the ways in which the movements of the self or soul in pursuit of the finality of God's purpose and love can serve as an apt model for the literacies fundamental to becoming theologically adept and astute. It is also to address some of the means by which theological librarianship can more fruitfully participate in and foster the development of these literacies for its students. There are two movements at work in the process outlined by Augustine that at first glance might seem paradoxically opposite. The first concerns the direction and trajectory toward which we are naturally moving to an intended end–a movement which must inevitably move one from their initial location to a new and more proper place and therefore must also take that person beyond or outside of their original selves toward another place and self where they will find their truest rest and purpose. This necessarily engages a person in theological education as *transformation,* which will be discussed as a key aspect of theological literacy. The second movement requires our human *will and commitment* to adhere to, and not place obstacles in the way of, the direction that is set before us. Augustine wrote passionately of this challenge grounded in his own life experiences. "I was in the external world and sought you there, and in my unlovely state I plunged into those lovely created things which you made. You were with me, and I was not with you. The lovely things kept me far from you" (*Confessions* 10.27.38), which conveys the sense of a choice or decision to be made. Whereas one's loving is a given, the object of one's love is not. "Love as much as you like," Augustine counseled, "but take care what you love" (*Expositions of the Psalms* 31[2].5). The movement toward the love of God as our intended place of rest requires a concerted act of the will in opposition to other loves one might pursue. These two movements together should be considered essential to becoming theologically literate in the context of formal theological education in our times: *the movement of transformation* beyond one's initial selfhood and *the movement of commitment and fidelity* toward attaining one's ultimate intended end. It is these dual objectives that distinguish theological literacy and education from all other academic endeavors–what the Catholic theologian David Tracy (2002, 15) has described as the systematic bringing together of "action and thought, academy and church, faith and reason, the community of inquiry and the community of commitment and faith."

The need to reconsider the meaning and purpose of theological education and literacy becomes especially imperative in light of a 2015 Lilly Endowment-funded project entitled *Theological Education Between the Times* that sought, through a series of consultations, the assessments from nearly sixty theological educators across a wide and deeply diverse spectrum of institutions and faith traditions on the current state of theological education and its hopes and expectations for the future. The project's guiding precept characterized being "between the times" in relation to the dramatic changes occurring in schools, churches, and the wider society, pointing to "a time of transition from one prevailing paradigm in theological education to another." The project also identified the "professional model" of theological education, which stressed the formation of ministers as professionals with the requisite skills and knowledge in the standard theological disciplines, as having been the prevailing pedagogical norm for more than a century. That "professional constellation of institutions, ideas, and individual life courses is breaking up," the study contends, and "it is not yet clear what will replace it." What is needed in a time of rapid and profound cultural change is the capacity to discern anew "signs of God's activity" and work in the world, enabling us to craft creative and faithful responses and leading us to new forms of discipleship (Smith, Jewell, and Kang 2018, 1-9).

The project's participants did not come to any conclusions about one model or vision of theological education that should be the guiding *telos* for all. This chapter also does not seek to hold forth a blueprint for theological education and literacy to which all institutions in our sharply multivalent culture should ascribe. My viewpoints are in many respects representative of my experiences as the director of a theological library and faculty member in church history at a seminary of the Roman Catholic Church–the University of Saint Mary of the Lake–whose principal stated mission is ito "prepare candidates for the diocesan priesthood" and to provide "initial, post-graduate or ongoing formation for priests and those who collaborate with them in ministry." Formation as a crucial aspect of preparation for ministry, as others have noted, tends in its emphasis to set Roman Catholic seminaries apart from their Protestant counterparts. Within the Catholic tradition, theological education itself is defined as a process of formation. As expressed in the United States' Conference of Catholic Bishops' (USCCB) *Program for Priestly Formation*, "Formation, as the Church understands it, is not equivalent to a secular sense of schooling or, even less, job training. Formation is first and foremost cooperation with the grace of God" (USCCB 2006, 28). A related document from the USCCB (2001) explains how, when "moved by that grace... we make ourselves available to God's work of transformation. And that making ready a place for the Lord to dwell in us and transform us we call formation." Augustine, as bishop to his fourth-century North African churches, shared similar concerns about the need to prepare able and dedicated pastors.[2] It is therefore perhaps not coincidental that both he and today's American Catholic leadership have identified formation as the key to readying persons for pastoral ministry and have defined this as a movement within the individual: one, toward cooperation or *fidelity* to the grace and love of God; and two, as *trans*formation that becomes available through our movement toward faith and in turn leads us toward that "place" God intends for us. Formation of this nature identifies and seeks to build upon the "vital connection" between pastors' identities and what they will do as ministers; it is "the continuing integration of identity and function for the sake of [the church's] mission" (USCCB 2001).

Image 1: Mundelein Seminary student in the Saint John Paul II Chapel (© University of Saint Mary of the Lake, used with permission).

Literacy as Transformation

A focus on transformation as a key component of a formational model of theological education and literacy points to an openness to inquiry, to genuine conversation and dialogue with the abundance of voices past and present that we encounter, to an embrace of change through new possibilities, understandings, and experiences, to a willingness to let go of fears and apprehensions that inhibit us, and to full-fledged freedom of thinking. This broad conception of theological literacy invites a much more dynamic pedagogical participation among theological libraries and librarians, as it extends well beyond explications of information literacy in academic library pedagogy that emphasize knowledge and mastery of the fundamental tools, technologies, and resources necessary to access and produce written information. The critical thinking skills that are stressed as central to this pedagogy are those that enable students to coherently navigate and utilize the copious amounts of information at hand–designing appropriate search strategies, identifying and discerning proper sources, evaluating the reliability or quality of these sources, and using them effectively in making arguments and composing independent research. The ACRL's paradigmatic *Framework for Information Literacy* (2016) does encourage innovation and openness in academic inquiry, particularly in its sixth conceptual "frame" where it advocates "Strategic Exploration" that is "nonlinear," encourages "mental flexibility and creativity," and utilizes divergent as well as convergent modes of thinking.

This standard is different in degree, however, from the claim by pedagogical philosopher Paulo Freire (1974), for example, that literacy should be an act of self-emancipation. Freire's liberationist concerns seek to address the plight of those individuals and communities who have been heretofore embedded in oppressive sociopolitical environments and to utilize the methods of literacy as a means of lifting them out of their oppression. Although forged in an entirely different context, theological literacy in its ideal form should also be conceived as an emancipatory process by which one is moving beyond or out of embedded faith tradition, gaining new knowledge and modes of learning, developing a more profound self-identity, and taking responsibility for and trusting what one has newly come to know. Movement away from this embeddedness can in fact be viewed as a critical step in becoming theologically literate. Psychologist Robert Kegan (1994, 103–6) has claimed that, until recently, an individual's embeddedness in their cultural environment ensured that they could function well on an "adolescent" level of moral consciousness; the uniformity and familiarity of their surroundings entailed that they did not need to expand developmentally beyond this. The rise of tremendous cultural diversity and heterogeneity with conflicting values concerning the most fundamental issues of human life has significantly altered the ability to remain comfortably embedded in our social milieus.

One's faith traditions and religious life can often, of course, be an essential facet of one's cultural embeddedness. How we arrive at an understanding of the meaning of our faith–of what it means to be a Christian–often develops within us from our earliest formative experiences, much like learning a language. From countless daily encounters with what the church says and does, and from contact and involvement with others in our homes, churches, and broader communities, our embedded theological thinking is the *implicit* theology deeply in place that Christians live out in their daily lives. This includes the theological messages intrinsic to and communicated by praying, preaching, worshipping, hymn singing, liturgy, personal conduct, and social action–everything that people say and do in the name of their faith.

The ability to move beyond the innate or inherited religious practices, communities, relationships, values, understandings, and mores through which one was formed thus becomes a critical component in developing a more profound level of theological literacy or vibrant consciousness about one's life of faith. It is this probing, transformative, self-aware form of literacy that should be encouraged and cultivated in the context of theological education. For theological librarians and other educators who are tasked with teaching courses in theological research and writing, it is important to grasp that in order to teach students to research and write theologically they must first be fundamentally able to *think* theologically. This has been described by one recent text in theological education as the movement from an embedded to a deliberative mode of theological thinking–a skill or gift that is much more difficult to attain and can be more troubling or disturbing as well, as it generally involves moving beyond prior settled convictions and understandings. Our embedded theologies seem natural, familiar, and comfortable to us, and we carry them within us for years, often unquestioned and even unspoken. Situations can arise, however, or circumstances can change which lead us to a reconsideration of our previous theological suppositions and to subject these to serious re-analysis and reflection. This moves us into the transformative realm of deliberative theology, an understanding of our faith that emerges from the process of carefully reflecting upon embedded theological convictions or the implicit understandings enmeshed in the life of faith. Feelings, memories, and preconceptions are often set aside or reevaluated in order to discover new insights that our narrower and more intensely personal views might have inhibited. Deliberative theological thinking questions what had previously been taken for granted, pressing beneath the surface to examine alternative understandings, seeking that which is most satisfactory and reformulating the meaning of faith as clearly and coherently as possible (Stone and Duke 2006, 13–20).

How, then, does one acquire this level of transformational theological literacy? In one sense, it is already manifest in those who have elected to engage in formal theological education. This is a self-selected vast minority within our modern culture who, by enrolling in a theological course of study have for the most part identified themselves as having moved beyond their earlier embedded practices, concepts, and customs and displayed a willingness or open-mindedness to progress toward a more deliberative theological mindset. I regularly teach courses in theological research and composition to first-year seminarians at Mundelein Seminary, and one of the first assignments that I generally request of them is to write a reflection paper that describes the nature, character, and sources of their embedded religious faith, and then to identify, if they can, a time or circumstance in their lives when they sensed themselves moving toward a more deliberative mode of theologizing. The occasions of this transformative movement vary to be sure. Some have written of a moment of trial or crisis that led to questions and doubts about their faith for which their embedded understandings had not fully prepared them or seemed inadequate. Others have described more of a gradual unfolding of an impulse within them or a conscientiousness that compels their efforts to seek a deeper understanding of their faith and to live out their Christian witness in well-informed and responsible ways, which has ultimately led to their following a calling to become priests. In whatever manner students may have arrived at this point, in all cases they share in this movement toward innovation and openness to new or different ways of thinking and seeing. I will often refer in my classes to the scriptural model of the apostle Paul, who wrote of himself and others in a highly authentic manner in 1 Corinthians 13:12, "For now we see in a mirror dimly, but then face to face. Now I know in part; then I shall understand fully, even as I have been fully understood." These students' election to move toward becoming more diligent and deliberative theological thinkers is a step toward seeing and understanding their lives of faith more clearly through deepening, broadening, enriching, and possibly revising their initial understandings by critical analysis concerning their character and adequacy. It is only the next step, however, in the lengthy and intricate movement toward attaining our ultimate end as people of faith–more fully knowing and being known by the divine.

Seminary students, as well as other Christian seekers, will often find themselves at different points along a continuum between the poles of embedded and deliberative theological thinking. Some may experience the shift toward a deliberative mode as a sharp or hard and conflicted break from their past embeddedness. More often, these two ways of thinking and being theologically merge together or overlap, and the boundaries between them can be difficult to discern or even indistinct. While theological students may have set themselves apart in their move toward the pole of deliberative thought, eschewing the tendency of most others to adhere more closely to the familiar, predictable, and desirable in our embedded thinking, they now face a daunting challenge and difficult work in moving further along this path. For one, those who set out in this direction don't quite know where it may lead. They may hope and anticipate that it will be an enjoyable, meaningful, and inspiring experience, but that's not a certainty. Distancing oneself from embedded understandings of faith and subjecting these to searching examination can be an arduous and painful task. It tends to bring to an end, or at least lead to a diminishment of, our previous foundations and assurances that provided stability and cohesion and formed our self-identity–a disquieting experience of incertitude to which Christian mystics and theologians through the centuries referred in expressive and graphic imagery such as "a dark night of the soul" or a sojourn in the "wilderness" (Stone and Duke 2006, 20–5).

For those, then, who have chosen through their engagement in theological education to take on this challenging and transformative task, that which is needed foremost is a self-conscious receptivity to new thoughts and ideas that leads to participation in an extensive inherited conversation. This is at the heart of becoming engaged in the community of inquiry that defines academic education. To become educated, David Tracy (2002, 13-14) observes, is "to be freed to enter the conversation of all the living and dead." Tracy further claims that, in order to genuinely enter this critical conversation, one must let go of whatever it is that has inhibited one from taking part before–a liberating process that allows us to truly listen and question, to enable our thoughts and opinions to be examined and tested, to discover fresh possibilities, and to encounter a myriad of novel understandings and experiences that become available when we are open to them.

Entry into this inherited conversation is especially vital in relation to theological literacy and education. The Christian tradition has thrived, developed, and adapted during all its centuries largely through its capacity to embrace an authentic, critical community of inquiry that informs and shapes it. Each generation is called upon to reconceive and re-form the tradition they have inherited in ever-changing circumstances that reflect and respond to their unique contexts. The ability to participate in this ongoing, perpetual conversation that extends well before and beyond us is thus a crucial part of deliberative or critical theological thinking. Those who are intent on some form of ministry or Christian service will be expected, in response to their calling, to provide a public witness or testimony of their faith, to contribute their part toward the conversation that defines and enfolds them. The theological understanding and Christian witness one attains through deliberative thinking is uniquely one's own. Yet it is a faith and set of convictions deeply shared by others, addressing common themes and issues, and drawing upon a common stock of theological concepts and resources (the language of faith)–points of connection that enable others to identify and acknowledge one's theology as distinctively "Christian." One's individual theologizing hence also bears the responsibility of contributing to the Christian faith and its people's well-being, each person's contribution enlivening and enriching the conversation as a whole.

Image 2: Mundelein Seminary students studying in McEssy Theological Resource Center (© University of Saint Mary of the Lake, used with permission).

Literacy as Engagement in an Extended Conversation

To participate in and contribute to this conversation in the theological community of inquiry therefore requires first being informed and made knowledgeable *by* this conversation. Anglican theologian Alister McGrath (2017) has noted that "it is virtually impossible to do theology as if it had never been done before... [there is] always an element of looking over one's shoulder to see how things were done in the past, and what answers were then given" in order to illumine and provide answers to current questions and issues. "To serve the community of today," Karl Barth (1963, 42) expressed in similar fashion, "theology itself must be rooted in the community of yesterday." Theological understanding and discourse are developed in conversation with prior sources that provide us with present resources, and the theological library becomes, to be sure, a central locus for this conversational encounter. Fundamental knowledge about these sources is not the final objective of deliberative theological thinking, however. Barth wrote in another place (2011, 216) that the founders of the faith, "in their seeking, questioning, confusion, and affliction... could challenge us to become founders *ourselves,* also responding to *our* time." True participation in and contribution to the extended conversation demands the appropriation of the sources one consults through an independent critical lens, or a *dynamic integration* between the sources studied and one's own creative thought whereby one can discern truth and meaning through engagement in the conversation while also seeking to discover and express one's authentic self relative to one's own personal context. The theological librarian, I would maintain, through courses, workshops, and individual conversations on theological research and literacy, is in a distinctive position in being able to guide students in identifying and then appropriating the sources they study in ways that integrate their independent, critical, and authentic thinking.

How, then, does one determine the appropriate conversation partners for one's particular form of deliberative theological thinking? The response to this question often leads to a highly personalized engagement within the extended theological conversation, and this is again an area in which theological library instructors can assist students in identifying their prior conversation partners as well as those with whom they they might engage in the present and future. Essays received from my seminary students on the sources of their embedded theologies have vividly, and not surprisingly, illustrated the significant influences of those close to them, family members both immediate and extended, in sharing and passing on the theological understandings gained from their own life experiences. This points to the larger truth that many, if not most, voices who might have something to contribute to this conversation are also never or barely heard outside their own immediate, very narrow sphere. A large-scale effort to rectify this yawning void has been undertaken in recent decades in embracing other voices of interpretation that had long been excluded from the theological conversation, transforming this into a more participatory, inclusive, and global dialogue among those who enter into it. The objective of theological literacy and education should be to continually expand the circle of conversation partners with which we engage, for limiting or restricting this is the nascent seminarian theologian's, and thus the church's, loss. Theological literacy requires an engagement with the horizons of Christian diversity across time, traditions, and cultures. It should be the objective of the theological librarian to expand these conversational horizons both through their personal interactions and consultations with students as well as through collection development practices that can provide and often introduce students to new voices and resources, enriching an ever-evolving theological discourse.

This essential pegadogical goal raises a unique curricular challenge for theological institutions in our current academic environment, however, in defining what makes a theological student literate. Theological education has traditionally sought to maintain a balance between what has been termed as *critical* (the ability to read and write about theological ideas, often in dialogue with non-theological methods and disciplines) and *practical* (utilizing theological ideas as a basis for religious praxis) literacy, or what has also been described as the distinction between knowledge *about* and knowledge of *how* in relation to one's faith tradition. Yet this is an integrative balance facing increasing obstacles, whose plausibility and direction for the future of theological institutions is being questioned amid the challenges and possibilities of a rapidly pluralizing culture.[3]

Theological education in its recent Western context has characteristically been focused principally on the dimension of critical literacy–on knowledge *about* that presupposes but may only be loosely associated with knowledge of *how*. One reason for this can be discerned in John Paul II's encyclical letter *Fides et ratio* (1998), in which he famously proclaims, in his opening statement of greeting and blessing, the essential unity of faith and reason working together "like two wings on which the human spirit rises to the contemplation of the truth... And God has placed in the human heart a desire to know the truth," he writes, "in a word, to know himself–so that, by knowing and loving God, men and women may also come to the fullness of truth about themselves." On the one hand, the Christian tradition has sought through the centuries to identify and define itself over and against the conventions and norms of the prevailing socio-historical context. It has been attentive and responsive to the manifold cultural challenges to it, and it has sought to form faithful disciples who in certain respects transcend and are not defined by the cultures and societies in which they live. At the same time, however, Christian tradition seeks to make universal claims about itself as embodying a revelatory, objective truth that applies and is accessible to all peoples and cultures across time and space, as John Paul II acknowledged.

To make claims to universality of this nature that are persuasive and have relevance beyond an enclosed and private parochialism requires an engagement with the larger intellectual culture, and especially with the efforts of other disciplines and fields of study to identify objective, universal truths. Recently canonized Roman Catholic theologian John Henry Newman similarly stated it as his goal "to find the means, by which, the training of the mind and unity of [universal knowledge] understood as a good in itself, could be given life and power in a way that would be congruent also with the prescriptions of faith and obedience" (1996, 78-9, 89-90). This has largely defined critical theological literacy as well as the nature and standards of curricula in theological education in the modern era, as they have striven to dialogue with and be informed by intellectual currents such as Enlightenment philosophical rationalism, social-historical criticism, and the scientific method in arriving at similar or opposite truths. The theological disciplines have found their conversation partners primarily within the secular academic realm, through the literary-historical-critical methods of the modern humanities and social sciences, the critiques of modern analytic philosophy, and, to a lesser degree, the methodologies of the natural sciences (Heim 2002, 59).

The ironic dilemma for theological education and literacy, as noted also in *Fides et ratio,* is that philosophy as well as other fields of study have in large part abandoned the belief in and search for universal truth. The academic community of inquiry, including literature, historical study, and the humanities and social sciences in general, have been reshaped by postmodern theory, which casts a shadow of cynicism if not outright negation upon any efforts at objectivity or universality and champions instead the culturally contextual, contingent, and localized character of all perspectives, actions, and developments. Religious studies scholars, for example, commonly draw a distinction between what is *real*—by which is meant particular experiences, practices, encounters, and beliefs that are not universally real but real *only for* local, circumscribed cultures or peoples—and what is *true,* which is determined unequivocally by empirical scientific or historical truth—e.g., that which occurs solely in naturalistic terms either through human agency or the operations of the natural world.

On this view, for the study of religion to be rigorously scientific and pure it must rid itself of all theological vestiges that are irredeemably tainted as being authoritarian, uncritical, and ideological.[4] From an opposing perspective, Orthodox theologian Vigen Guroian (2018, 17-20) speaks in a similar vein nonetheless of an "aggressive, monolithic secularism" that often rejects "transcendental reality, or at least regards the possibility that it exists as irrelevant to human endeavor... persuaded that the perfect or best of all possible worlds is a strictly human and historical project." Postmodernity, he argues, is "the empty shell" of a desacralized Christianity "inhabited by alien ideologies" that have a "certain predilection for the unknown, or 'secondary religiosity', after which complete secularity follows." The growing chasm between the academic interests and endeavors represented in departments of religious studies in colleges or universities and seminary programs of theological study often reflects this theoretical and polemical divide. Theological education today within institutions such as those in the Catholic tradition, whose principal goal is preparing students for ministry, can often find itself somewhat isolated within the broader academic community of inquiry in its adherence to the pursuit of ultimate, objective truths about God and human existence, including a fuller understanding of oneself in relation to God, as John Paul II described. [5]

Literacy as Formation for Leadership

Where then does the future lie for theological education and the disciplines that comprise it? Can its character and priorities be reconceived in a post-Christian age in a way that enables it to maintain its engagement in and contributions to the wider public of intellectual inquiry and discourse while also preserving its unique objectives and purposes in educating men and women for ordained and lay leadership in Christian ministries? Twentieth-century Roman Catholic theologian Romano Guardini (1998) maintained that the Christian faith's response to this age should be to "take on a new decisiveness" that would "strip itself of all secularism, all analogies with the secular world, all flabbiness and eclectic mixtures," and that Christians would find revitalization through "being forced to distinguish [themselves] more sharply from a dominantly non-Christian ethos" (quoted in Guroian 2018, 20-1). Without, perhaps, moving quite to that extreme, other creative directions for theological education can be found through the identification and incorporation of new conversation partners with which it can be engaged, embracing and espousing certain of these intellectual and cultural trends without being wholly subsumed by them. This circles us back to the need in theological education for integration between practical or applied literacy and the more "academic" disciplines (i.e., biblical studies, ethics or moral theology, systematic or dogmatic theology, and church history) that have traditionally been ascribed to critical modes of literacy and which have tended to take primacy of place in the theological curriculum. As the bonds of the theological-critical disciplines to the academic community of inquiry have been fragmented through the postmodern turn, this may be an opportune moment to reassert academic theology's traditional ties to the formational or spiritual emphases that define theological education uniquely apart from its counterparts in the academy. "Theological education crunches souls and moves hearts as much as it informs minds," observes Daniel O. Aleshire (2018, 26). Karl Barth's (1963) counsel that theological work can only be done "in the indissoluble unity of prayer and study" is illuminating in this context. "Prayer without study would be empty," he observed, and "study without prayer would be blind." The unifying nature of theological education is also pointed to in *Fides et ratio*, in John Paul II's description of the innate human desire and yearning for both the *knowledge* and *love* of God–and ourselves.

This unity of academic and spiritual dimensions should therefore be an essential feature of holistic programs in theological education, with each playing an equivalent role in the transformative experience of students. Knowledge about the various theological disciplines, however sophisticated and profound, cannot be an end in itself for those whose ultimate objective is to be a spiritual leader in their own faith communities. Skills in critical thinking and literacy should be purposed toward attaining a practical fluency that enables students to understand and respond to the spiritual and psychological needs they will encounter, to be able to stand before a congregation and speak on hard matters or stand beside a family in times of grief and sorrow or be pastorally present at the sacred moments and experiences in people's lives. Augustine maintained that the ability of a pastoral leader "derives more from his devotion to prayer than his dedication to oratory... by praying for himself and for those he is about to address, he must become a man of prayer before becoming a man of words" (*De doctrina christiana* 4.15.32). Education in the traditional theological disciplines supports and is supported by spiritual formation and practice in the means by which one's education and formation are to be enacted in the ministries of the church.

In reconceiving programs for theological literacy in the current postmodern and post-Christian context, one should therefore consider transformative engagement with those disciplines, courses of study, and conversation partners that will be most likely to benefit and enhance the formation of students toward religious leadership and service in their communities. Theological libraries and librarians should be accorded an important place in this discussion, as it will enable them to better guide their collection development practices in these new directions as well as craft their education and instruction programs in ways that take into account the newer research resources and foci for study in pastoral leadership. I will note here some of the recent curricular emphases that have been identified in reshaping theological education in ways that can give it new meaning, vitality, and relevance in dialogue with the larger twenty-first century world.

One is a renewed focus on ecumenical studies in its interdenominational or intra-Christian dimensions. The massive trends toward globalization in modern society and the resulting tremendously diverse culture in which we live presents challenge and opportunity for the Christian tradition. In the face of such frequently non-Christian diversity, it becomes increasingly important for Christians of different faith communities to be able to perceive and understand themselves in more unified ways that bridge the tensions and oppositions that have long differentiated them–to resemble more the church catholic and universal it has historically professed and aspired to be. Theological education can assist toward that end by modeling in its curricula, to the extent possible, the objective of comprehensive access to the full breadth and depth of the Christian faith's resources across time, geographic space, and traditions. Theological literacy in this ecumenical vein mandates a fundamental level of knowledge about Christian belief and practice as it is understood and carried forth in the various other communions of the Christian church. Pastoral leaders should be able to better comprehend and value the full richness of faith expressions that comprise the universal church, so that they may be well-positioned to interpret and apply these expressions in relation to their own faith communities and also be more equipped to guide their church members to those Christian resources and practices that will best assist them in their faith development, even if these may be outside of their own particular traditions strictly speaking (Heim 2002, 63–4). As an example of this ecumenical thrust, the University of St. Mary of the Lake, while a seminary of the Roman Catholic Church, makes a concerted effort also to educate and familiarize its students with regard to the traditions, liturgies, and theologies of the Eastern Orthodox Church in its various historical manifestations. The seminary also encourages student and faculty participation through joint coursework in a local ecumenical association, the Northside Chicago Theological Institute, comprised of five seminaries that seek to include a variety of theological perspectives: Roman Catholic, Eastern Orthodox, Protestant, and Jewish. The seminar offered in the fall of 2019 was on "Global Theologies: How the Growth of the Church within the Majority World is Affecting Theology."

A curricular focus on interfaith relations affords, similarly to ecumenism, an opportunity for future pastoral leaders to forge more vital and meaningful connections and conversations with the complex societies in which they'll be ministering. The globalization of modern culture elicits a pressing need to be able to explain one's faith traditions to an increasingly non-Christian population. The relationship of Christianity to other religious faiths is a convoluted one, and schools of theology today will differ as to thcone proper methods and approaches to follow. In all cases, however, theological literacy should entail the capacity to communicate a Christian witness for one's faith to those who do not share it. To be effective in this type of communication requires sufficient knowledge of these other faiths and their stance toward or critiques of Christianity to be able to conduct an authentic dialogue that is not one-sided but interactive, reciprocal, and mutually beneficial in gaining an understanding of one another. Seminary degree program standards of education have been introduced that require ministerial competency "in the multi-faith and multicultural context of contemporary society." Here, too, theological libraries and librarians can assume a prominent role in adopting collections practices and implementing instructional programs that strive to familiarize and educate students more fully concerning the resources of the universal church and non-Christian faiths. In a time of notable budget austerities for both seminaries and their libraries, it can be a daunting challenge to find a means for allocating significant funds for resources outside of one's own institutional traditions, beliefs, and practices, but efforts should be made nonetheless. Becoming well-informed about other faith traditions through interreligious pedagogy and literacy can help in forming the mature intellectual and spiritual identities of a Christian minister, enabling one to better define, understand, deepen, and live out one's own faith commitments and sense of vocation within a religiously plural society (Alexander 2018, 49, 58-9).[6]

A key element in developing a more profound ecumenical and interreligious literacy in theological education is an expansion of our conceptions and representations concerning what constitutes Christianity and the Christian church in the present era. The shift of Christianity's pre-eminence and influence to the global South and East (Africa, Latin and South America, Asia)–or the "majority world"–has been well-documented. To what extent theological literacy and education should seek to address and incorporate this reality in its programs of study is much less certain and often not significantly considered. Yet as the churches of these regions continue to generate a profusion of theological literature and scholarship that conveys the unique languages, conceptions, and practices of their faith, theological institutions in North America should at least take up the question of whether the contributions of these faith communities are to be included in the resources and curricula that are offered in redefining what it means to be theologically literate. One possible connective force in this context, justifying a greater emphasis on study of these global Christianities, would be the resonances as well as dissimilarities found between these faith communities and the racially and ethnically-oriented Christian communities in North America (African, Hispanic, Asian) that are increasingly well-represented in theological education. While often embodying very different backgrounds and cultural identities than the emerging churches on other continents, many seminary students from these as well as other faith communities might find studies of this nature informative and insightful in presenting a broader portrait of world Christianities today, especially in connection with their intended ministries in local churches that mirror this racial and/or ethnic composition. Multicultural faith perspectives that enable North American theological schools to engage in conversation and bridge their religious and socio-cultural distances with the global Christian church may soon become an important facet of theological education and literacy (Heim 2002, 64-5).

Beyond wholescale curricular changes in these newer areas of theological study, which are often difficult given the lack of resources and opportunity in an already over-extended seminary curriculum, there are other programmatic means of introducing ecumenical, interreligious, and global aspects of Christianity to seminary students. Mundelein Seminary, for example, has in the past couple of years convened on its campus the National Muslim Catholic Dialogue conference, as well as more recently held a symposium of African Catholic theologians on the topic of "Joseph Ratzinger and the Future of African Theology." An important place for theological librarianship also exists in this context in augmenting collections in these specialized areas that are likely not too well-established, as well as conducting workshops or other instructional sessions on the use of these resources. The ability to pool together and utilize emerging technologies to provide for a genuine global sharing of open access library resources would be an additional invaluable contribution of Western theological institutions and libraries toward conjoining the worldwide Christian church in unity and fellowship, the growth and maturation of which in its vibrancy and fullness would belong, and be of benefit, to all.

Image 3: Conference on Joseph Ratzinger and the Future of African Theology, sponsored by the Center for Scriptural Exegesis, Philosophy and Doctrine at the University of Saint Mary of the Lake in collaboration with the Benedict XVI Institute for Africa, October 17-19, 2019 (© University of Saint Mary of the Lake, used with permission).

Another very different avenue of curricular development that has the potential to redefine theological education and literacy is to be found within the disciplines of the hard or natural sciences. The complex relationship of religion or faith to the various fields of science has witnessed an explosion of interest and written scholarship in recent years, and this is certainly a burgeoning and dynamic area for collection development and literacy instruction in theological libraries. How the concepts and theories of the sciences can be integrated into formal programs in theological studies is a challenge that has not been fully resolved. To the extent this is feasible, the key pedagogical questions must concern how these scientific insights can better equip one for pastoral leadership in the local life of the church. Mundelein Seminary, for example, recently received through its rector and president Fr. John Kartje a grant from the John Templeton Foundation to encourage scientific literacy and the integration of theology and science in the formation of Catholic seminarians. The Templeton Grant was awarded through the Science in Seminaries Initiative at John Carroll University, whose express goal is to "recover and reintegrate the tradition of teaching scientific literacy in the seminary intellectual formation program." It is an initiative that clearly re-envisions the purposes and character of theological education in our contemporary context, anticipating "a clergy prepared to engage the bigger questions of science that are foundational for effective evangelization in a scientific and technological world." Mundelein Seminary also aspires to build upon the Templeton project through the endowment of a Center for Faith and Science.

Of course, the scientific disciplines are tremendously varied in their nature and purposes and thus in their suitability for incorporation into theological education. Studies in the cognitive or neurophysiological sciences as applied to psychological insights for pastoral counseling are one possible candidate, as are evolutionary psychology in relation to matters of personal and social behavior and more refined anthropological conceptions of what it means to be human through an analysis of ethical issues like artificial intelligence, genetic engineering, and biotechnologies. Engagement in current cutting-edge scientific debates about the origins of life and the universe that hold theological import might also be beneficial in preparing students for openly discussing the intricacies of these ideas and concepts within their congregations (Heim 2002, 65–6).

The various disciplinary and curricular emphases outlined briefly here can be a means of reconceiving and reinterpreting theological education and literacy in meaningful and compelling ways in the postmodern era. Undergirding each of these potential new academic engagements, however, is formation for theological and pastoral leadership as the lynchpin by which all pedagogical considerations should be measured. Schools of theology have traditionally viewed as their principal task the education in critical literacy that has been discussed, in close consort with the broader academic community of inquiry. Practical literacy, or the molding of one's spirituality and character to become a spiritual leader in the church, was largely perceived as something to be attained and nurtured through one's own faith community either prior to or as a part of ministerial service. It is one thing, however, to be well-educated and knowledgeable in the theological disciplines; it is another altogether to have not only a mind but a heart and spirit for Christian pastoral leadership. Daniel Aleshire (2018, 32–6) presents this as a distinctively Christian *habitus,* a way of perceiving, responding to, and being in the world that involves both patterns of thinking and living. This type of personal formation, he contends, should be central, and not co-curricular or secondary, in programs of theological education. Augustine likewise asserted that the pastor's "way of life becomes, in a sense, an abundant source of eloquence" (*De doctrina christiana* 4.29.61). Theological literacy and education are purposed to equip students vocationally to be steadfast Christian leaders for a lifetime. Theological institutions that do not place a strong emphasis on formation as an integral component of the educational program and its resources, including those of the theological library, are abdicating an essential aspect of this preparation, whose objective should be to form not only educated but *committed* and *faithful* leaders of the Christian church. Informed theological reasoning and reflection, sacramental and liturgical life, and spiritual formation should be conceived as mutually interdependent aspects of the one reality as a Christian minister that connects the whole person with God–to be "grafted onto Christ," as the Catholic bishop Robert Barron (2020) writes, "and hence drawn into the very dynamics of the inner life of God."

Literacy as an Act of Will and Love

This brings us back full circle to the second element of St. Augustine's characterization of weight as love that I cited earlier in the chapter. Augustine was very cognizant of the difficulties in avoiding temptations and distractions that might inhibit one on the course toward attaining their ultimate end of happiness in God. To reach this end requires our abiding will and commitment to persevere and move forward in the face of numerous deterrent forces. He often characterized one's efforts to fully love and become one with God as a "pilgrimage" that was demanding and strenuous but also a destination of complete fulfillment for those who remained true. The key to success on this pilgrim's path was placing love of God above all other lesser loves–our love of good and beautiful but "lower things." A principal concern of Augustine's, in setting forth the character of this pilgrimage, rested again in preparing skilled ministers of the church. In *De doctrina christiana,* he stated forthrightly in the last paragraph of this text his purpose in writing it: "to set out to the best of my poor ability, not what sort of pastor I am myself, lacking many of the necessary qualities as I do, but what sort the pastor should be who is eager to toil away, not only for his own sake but for others, in the teaching of sound, that is of Christian, doctrine" (4.31.64).

Augustine illustrates in this passage the importance in Christian formation for ministry of being educated in correct Christian doctrine, sufficiently to be able to teach it to others, which would seem to correspond largely with aspects of the critical literacy in theological education that have been discussed. Preceding or providing the foundation for this knowledge acquisition, however, are two crucial personality or character traits noted by Augustine: 1) an *eagerness* or *love* for the ministry that perseveres no matter the hardships; and 2) a willingness or commitment to *serve others* in a community of faith. For Augustine, theological literacy and education must be about more than the knowledge that comes through engagement in the theological community of inquiry and a facility with the discourses, methods, and sources of theological study if it is to attain its truest end of forming persons for ministry. In my personal experience as a theological library director and faculty member, I have observed that those who attend theological schools often do so with the explicit intent of being formed to be faithful leaders in communities of faith. The knowledge they gain through their studies they yearn to apply as teachers and preachers, worship and liturgical leaders, counselors, caregivers, and healers to congregants searching and praying for answers to life's most pressing questions.

The critical question, then, for programs in theological education and literacy concerns how they can assist and guide students in this endeavor, effectively forming them for the ministries in which they will engage. And how can theological libraries and librarians meaningfully contribute to this extensive and far-reaching formational process, which admittedly lies outside the purview of most academic library objectives? Augustine's counsel in *De doctrina christiana* provides us with a basic twofold method. The first step is to encourage and cultivate the eagerness and love for ministry they are seeking for their lives, to nurture them in being formed spiritually as Christian leaders-to-be, to enliven within them and build upon a vibrant personal faith while also challenging them to strive toward a deeper, more prayerful life of faith, and ultimately to enable them toward full experience of that profound love of God displacing all other loves that Augustine stressed as necessary to reach our pilgrimage's end. Attaining this level of spiritual maturity and wholeness is not a simple or easy development; it often demands some form of personal conversion and renewal on the part of seminarians. Augustine wrote frequently of Christian salvation in a discourse of health and healing–a restoration from "this devastating disease in the souls of men and women" whose cure required a cleansing of our transgressions (*Expositions of the Psalms* 18[2].15). It must also be a continual healing process, for "the mind itself, in which by nature our reason and intelligence abide," is "weakened by certain darkening and long-standing faults, too weak to cling in enjoyment to the unchangeable light (of God)." It had to be renewed, strengthened, and healed day after day to become capable of such a blessed state, which meant "to be steeped in faith and cleansed" in order to "more confidently proceed toward the truth" (*De civitate Dei* 11.2.2).

In Augustinian theology, our ability to move in love toward God, in the face of our weaknesses and incapacities, depends upon God's initial movement in love toward us. We could not love God, Augustine acknowledged, "if he had not first loved us and made us lovers of him. For love comes from him." And again he wrote, "Man has no capacity to love God except from God" (*The Trinity* 15.31). According to this conception, God's love for us stirs deeply in us a desire to more fully *love* and *know* God. In this we see the integration of love and knowledge, or faith and the rational mind. Faith seeks understanding; "yearning is the bosom of the heart... we shall understand if we extend our yearning as far as we can" (*Homilies on the Gospel of John* 40.10).[7] To grasp what is true, we must continually seek to expand upon our longings for God's love. For Augustine, the formation of pastors for ministry, and thus the character of theological education, should embrace a wide range of our godly desires and yearnings, each of which sheds its own light on the truth of God. "This is what the divine scriptures do for us," he proclaimed, "what the assembly of the people does for us, what the celebration of the sacraments, holy baptism, hymns in praise of God, and my own preaching do for us; all this yearning is not only sown and grows in us, but it also increases to such a capacity that it is ready to welcome what eye has not seen, nor has ear heard, nor has it entered the heart of man," to be able to receive, in other words, the unanticipated and unforeseen gifts of God's grace that are open to those who strive in these ways to grow in knowledge and love of him (*Homilies on the Gospel of John* 40.10).

In Augustine's model for preparing the pastorate we thus observe the coalescence of critical and practical literacy–of knowledge *about* and knowledge of *how*—each of which serves the unified pedagogical goal of interconnecting one's knowledge and love of God. Only as we develop and refine our longing for God in the many ways we can, intellectually as well as through formational practice, can we mature in our knowledge, experience, and understanding of God and his designs for us. It is this interconnective mode of theological education, an interwoven effort or fusion that connects the whole person to God in knowledge and love, which I would suggest as a means of revitalization for theological literacy, and theological librarianship's participation in this, in a postmodern culture that largely spurns the objectives and aspirations it holds.

There is one other essential aspect of a renewed theological literacy implicit in Augustine's description of the various means of devotion through which we seek to meet our desire for God. Other than the study of Scripture, all of those practices he cites–gathering for worship, celebration of the sacraments, congregational singing, and preaching–do not occur in isolation but within a communal context. This hearkens back to Augustine's second measure in *De doctrina christiana* of what should define a qualified pastor–that is, a commitment to serving others. A

Christian leader's knowledge and love of God can only be truly formed to reach its intended end through commitment to a communion of the faithful in which one lives out, builds upon, and sustains one's own faith through serving their needs. Augustine often commented in parallel terms of our need to grow in the knowledge and love of God and neighbor. "So it is God," he wrote, "who fires man to the love of God and neighbor when he has been given to him" (*The Trinity* 15.31). The maturation of our faith, love, and understanding is predicated in large part on engagement in forms of grace that are communal in nature. Augustine cautioned that love of God could not be superseded by love of neighbor. "Love of God comes first and the manner of loving him is clearly laid down, in such a way that everything else flows into it." Every human being "should be loved on God's account, and God should be loved for himself" (*De doctrina christiana* 1.26.27, 1.27.28). To do otherwise would be to risk forming other persons into idols on whom was bestowed a misdirected and distorted love that impeded our ability to relate to them with Christian love, as fellow pilgrims loved by and in need of God. At the same time, counsels Augustine, other persons could be a means of helping us on the path toward attaining our ultimate end of happiness with God. He drew a distinction in this context between "enjoyment" of what should be held fast to "in love for its own sake" and the "use" or application of something "to the purpose of obtaining what you (ultimately) love" (*De doctrina christiana* 1.4.4; Jenson 2019, 72). The pilgrimage Augustine describes toward the love and knowledge of God is necessarily one of communion and accompaniment with fellow pilgrims. One becomes more loving and knowledgeable as a Christian pastor through engagement in a community that nurtures faith and a true understanding of its teachings. An authentic spiritual leader is enabled to guide others to greater Christian knowledge and love because they are engaged in this same prayerful seeking, receiving in the process of giving and sharing one another's burdens. The highest expression of Christian ministry, as Augustine conceived it, is a radical self-gifting, or love for the sake of the other. This comes through the movement of the committed theological student, as this chapter has illustrated, toward transformation of life and gift of self, through which one is able to share and participate most fully in the love and knowledge of God.

It is in one's Christian ministries, therefore, that the quality and depth of their theological literacy and education in all the dimensions we have discussed becomes most fully realized and revealed. The ultimate determination of the extent to which one has become theologically literate rests in one's ability to stand before one's believing and practicing community–the true *locus theologicus*—and effectively interpret, articulate, and apply theological learning to the life of the people, addressing and responding to their deepest Christian needs and yearnings. This demands a Christian wisdom, sensibility, perceptiveness, spiritual awareness or disposition, and quality of being that can be hard to pinpoint as to its source for those who have attained it, for formational theological development of this sort can be gained in many ways throughout one's theological education–both within the classroom and without, through one's academic reading and study in the library or in private reflection, in communal worship settings, small-group gatherings, or personal prayer, in ministry encounters or informal conversations. It is often a tangible part of the character or fabric of a theological institution–an educational ethos that permeates all singular academic or spiritual forms and experiences.

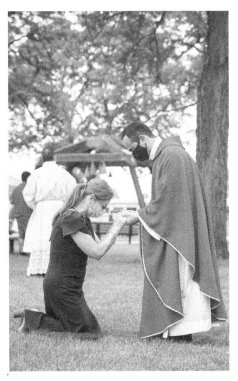

Image 4: Newly ordained priest from Mundelein Seminary offering blessings and prayer, July 10, 2020 (used by permission).

Mundelein Seminary, as noted previously, is comprised of several different formational elements, which together aspire to the goal for theological education and literacy I have portrayed in connecting the whole person to God in knowledge and love for the service of God's people. The four interwined components–human, intellectual, spiritual, and pastoral formation–hold as their unified objective the development of "true pastors, mature and holy, who will live, work, and pray with the people they serve in parish ministry" (Mundelein Seminary n.d.). The seminary's educational structure further reflects the primacy given to seminarian formation, as there is both a formation faculty, including advisors and spiritual directors, and an academic or teaching faculty who work closely and collaboratively together in their distinctive capacities to provide for the seminarian's preparation for ministry in the holistic sense I have described. The theological library and librarians can also be integral to the ministerial formation of students in both the more academic and intellectual or spiritual aspects of their education. This occurs through collection development and augmentation of resources that address newer as well as more traditional emphases in critical and practical literacy that have been discussed in this chapter. It can also frequently involve the offering of various forms of literacy instruction (e.g., courses, workshops, seminars, tutorials, and classroom sessions) that encompass aspects of these two modes of theological literacy.

The challenge for theological librarianship at Mundelein and elsewhere is that education for theological literacy has traditionally been seen almost exclusively within the realm of content provision and instruction in the utilization of the resources, tools, and technologies that foster theological research and study. To a certain extent, theological librarians can be expected to familiarize students with the content being studied sufficiently for their being able to design effective search methods or strategies as well as discern and evaluate appropriate, high-quality sources for their research projects. Even in this respect, however, the body of knowledge one acquires in order to navigate this content often comes largely outside of classes or instruction in theological literacy itself and within the various academic disciplines of theology proper. In considering the new curricular and disciplinary emphases I've cited, such as ecumenism, interfaith relations, global Christianities, and theology and the natural sciences, as well as the more traditional theological disciplines, I believe there should be more of a concerted effort in literacy instruction to fluently incorporate students' knowledge of the content on particular topics with their knowledge about how to proficiently access this content through the various library resources. Education in theological literacy in this vein, however, remains largely within the dimension of critical literacy or intellectual inquiry and has little bearing on the aspects of practical and formational literacy I have highlighted as intrinsic to students' theological and pastoral development. This largely corresponds with the ACRL's (2016) recent comprehensive reconceptualization of information literacy to focus on the cultivation of students' critical and analytical modes of thinking, grounded in a transdisciplinary set of "threshold concepts" that center on various dispositions and practices associated principally with knowledge acquisition.[8] Theological librarianship thus often finds itself at something of a pedagogical remove from both academic libraries and the larger program of seminary education. If, however, theological literacy and education are to be understood in the broad formational manner I have characterized–as an embrace and connection of the student in his or her entire personhood to God–then the literacy taught as an aspect of theological librarianship needs to be more fully incorporated within this more expansive vision. This should involve, following the Augustinian conception of readiness for Christian ministry, both a transformative movement in one's theological knowledge and self-understanding as well as spiritual development and commitment in faith to love of God and God's people.

A holistic paradigm for theological literacy and education may in fact invite a more participatory engagement of theological librarians in the preparation of students for ministry, as it strives to broaden conceptions of what this education should involve beyond the academic-critical inquiry and professionalization model of the traditional disciplinary framework. The emphasis in students' formation on the integration of intellectual knowledge and personal or spiritual maturation breaks down the distinctions between critical and practical literacy and thus opens new avenues for theological education that may at least give equal place to formational concerns. This could also allow instruction in theological literacy to be more integrated within the broader seminary program through collaborative pedagogical efforts and experiences–in co-taught, embedded, or online and blended courses that are part of a growing trend in theological curricula–whether the emphasis in these is more critical or formational in nature. This approach has the potential of conveying to students with greater clarity the ways in which the fundamental skills in critical thinking, research, and writing integral to theological literacy can be more concretely applied to their learning in particular disciplines and subjects–so that literacy is not simply something taught on an intellectual island.[9] One's own courses, workshops, or individual consultations with students as a theological librarian should also seek to value, understand, and engage with the broader formational conceptions I have discussed about what makes a student theologically literate. Integrative methods such as these can communicate and reflect the desired unities of theological education, both in terms of the unity of theological study across the disciplines–from academic-critical to practical-formational–as well as the larger unities that uniquely define theological education, as the conjoining of faith and understanding, mind and spirit, and the fullness of truth that comes through the knowledge and love of God. Ultimately the efficacy of this holistic model of theological literacy depends in large part upon the interest, motivation, and investment of the theological librarian committed to fully engaging with it and carrying it forward in all its transformative dimensions.

This is a vision and depth of literacy for theological education that is understandably scarcely addressed in the ACRL's redrawn standards for *information* literacy, as it necessarily involves more than attention to critical-analytical thinking skills and knowledge acquisition. It is, however, what makes theological literacy and librarianship unique and distinctive in relation to other forms of academic literacy. It is also what can define theological education powerfully apart from the broader academic community of inquiry that has largely turned away from its singular modes of thinking and being. As described by the Catholic theologian John Courtney Murray (1965, 4) in vivid terms in adopting a phrase from Blaise Pascal, theological study and learning "'takes us by the throat'" in engaging the whole person– "as intelligent and free, as a body, as a psychic apparatus, and a soul–an engagement whose personal nature touches every aspect of [our] conduct, character, and consciousness." A Presbyterian minister I have known has characterized the theological librarian in similarly evocative and expansive words as one who educates, equips, and prepares students with the resources they will need to be ministers to the people of God. It is this dynamic and fulsome conception of theological education, literacy, and librarianship, echoing Augustine's own convictions about love of God's grasp and direction of our whole being, that can serve as an apt model and guide for schools and libraries of theology today in forming students for ministry in a world that sorely needs their knowledge, love, and steadfast commitment.

Works Cited

Aleshire, Daniel O. 2018. "The Emerging Model of Formational Theological Education." *Theological Education* 51, no. 2: 25–38.

Alexander, Scott C. 2018. "Encountering the Religious 'Stranger': Interreligious Pedagogy and the Future of Theological Education." *Theological Education* 51, no. 2: 49–60.

Association of College and Research Libraries. 2016. *Framework for Information Literacy for Higher Education.* www.ala.org/acrl/standards/ilframework.

Augustine. 1991. *Confessions.* Translated by Henry Chadwick. Oxford: Oxford University Press.

——. 1995. *De doctrina christiana.* Translated by R. P. H. Green. Oxford: Clarendon Press.

——. 2005. *De civitate Dei.* Translated by P. G. Walsh. Cambridge: Aris & Phillips/Oxbow.

——. 2009. *Homilies on the Gospel of John.* Translated by Edmund Hill, O. P. Hyde Park, NY: New City Press.

——. 2015. *Essential Expositions of the Psalms.* Translated by Maria Boulding. Hyde Park, NY: New City Press of the Focolare.

Barron, Robert. 2020. *Daily Gospel Reflections*, January 3, 2020.

Barth, Karl. 1963. *Evangelical Theology: An Introduction*. Translated by Grover Foley. New York: Holt, Rinehart and Winston.

——. 2011. *Word of God and Theology*. Translated by Amy Marga. London: T&T Clark.

Freire, Paulo. 1974. *Pedagogy of the Oppressed*. Translated by Myra Bergman Ramos. New York: Seabury Press.

Guroian, Vigen. 2018. *The Orthodox Reality: Culture, Theology, and Ethics in the Modern World*. Grand Rapids, MI: Baker Academic.

Heim, S. Mark. 2002. "Renewing Ways of Life: The Shape of Theological Education." In *Theological Literacy for the Twenty-First Century*, edited by Rodney L. Petersen and Nancy M. Rourke, 55–67. Grand Rapids, MI: William B. Eerdman's Publishing Company.

Jenson, Matt. 2019. *Theology in the Democracy of the Dead: A Dialogue with a Living Tradition*. Grand Rapids, MI: Baker Academic Press.

John Paul II. 1998. *Fides et ratio*. Encyclical letter. *www.vatican.va/content/john-paul-ii/en/encyclicals/documents/hf_jp-ii_enc_14091998_fides-et-ratio.html*.

Kegan, Robert. 1994. *In Over Our Heads: The Mental Demands of Modern Culture*. Cambridge, MA: Harvard University Press.

McGrath, Alister. 2017. *Christian Theology: An Introduction*. Chichester, West Sussex, UK: Wiley-Blackwell.

Mundelein Seminary. n.d. *The Ten Aims of Mundelein Seminary Formation*. *usml.edu/mundelein-seminary/formation/walking-three-paths/*.

Murray, John Courtney, S. J. 1965. *The Problem of God*. New Haven, CT: Yale University Press.

Newman, John Henry. 1996. *The Idea of a University*. Edited by Frank M. Turner. New Haven, CT: Yale University Press.

Smith, Ted A., Marti R. Jewell, and S. Steve Kang. 2018. "A Special Issue with Essays from Theological Education Between the Times." *Theological Education* 51, no. 2: 1–9.

Stone, Howard W. and James O. Duke. 2006. *How to Think Theologically*. Minneapolis, MN: Fortress Press.

Tracy, David. 2002. "On Theological Education: A Reflection." In *Theological Literacy for the Twenty-First Century*, edited by Rodney L. Petersen and Nancy M. Rourke, 13–22. Grand Rapids, MI: William B. Eerdman's Publishing Company.

United States Conference of Catholic Bishops. 2001. *The Basic Plan for the Ongoing Formation of Priests*. *www.usccb.org/beliefs-and-teachings/vocations/priesthood/priestly-life-and-ministry/national-plan-for-the-ongoing-formation-of-priests.cfm*.

——. 2006. *Program of Priestly Formation*. Fifth edition. United States Conference of Catholic Bishops: Washington, DC.

Notes

1. For further recent discussion on this Augustinian theme, see Vincent Carraud, "*Pondus meum amor meus,* or Contradictory Self-Love," in *Augustine Our Contemporary: Examining the Self in Past and Present,* eds. Willemein Otten and Susan E. Schreiner (Notre Dame, IN: University of Notre Dame Press, 2018), 105–33; Joseph Torchia, "'*Pondus meum amor meus*': The Weight-Metaphor in St. Augustine's Early Philosophy," *Augustinian Studies* 21 (1990): 163–76.

2. Augustine's *De doctrina christiana* was intended to set forth the "necessary qualities" for strong and effective pastors.

3. For recent examples of this discourse on the purpose, nature, and priorities of theological education, see *Disruption and Hope: Religious Traditions and the Future of Theological Education,* ed. Barbara Wheeler (Waco, TX: Baylor University Press, 2019); Daniel O. Aleshire, *Earthen Vessels: Hopeful Reflections on the Work and Future of Theological Schools* (Grand Rapids, MI: William B. Eerdmans Pub., 2008); David H. Kelsey, *Between Athens and Berlin: The Theological Education Debate* (Eugene, OR: Wipf & Stock, 2011); Robert J. Banks, *Reenvisioning Theological Education: Exploring a Missional Alternative to Current Models* (Grand Rapids, MI: William B. Eerdmans Pub., 1999); David H. Kelsey, *To Understand God Truly: What's Theological about a Theological School?* (Louisville, KY: Westminster/John Knox Press, 1992); Max Stackhouse, *Apologia: Contextualization, Globalization, and Mission in Theological Education* (Grand Rapids, MI: William B. Eerdmans Pub., 1988); Edward Farley, *The Fragility of Knowledge: Theological Education in the Church and the University* (Philadelphia, PA: Fortress Press, 1988); Edward Farley, *Theologia: The Fragmentation and Unity of Theological Education* (Philadelphia, PA: Fortress Press, 1983).

4. Amy M. Hollywood of Harvard Divinity School discusses this postmodern critique of theology and Christianity while also largely adhering to it. Religion, according to this view, is necessarily a mere localized product of the human imagination. See her *Acute Melancholia and Other Essays: Mysticism, History, and the Study of Religion* (New York: Columbia University Press, 2016). Robert A. Orsi, a religious studies scholar at Northwestern University, offers a somewhat different rendering of the scholarly detachment intrinsic to the

academic study of religion and the distinction between localized and empirical truths or realities as an "in-between orientation, located at the intersection between self and the other" that is the object of one's study. See Robert A. Orsi, *Between Heaven and Earth: The Religious Worlds People Make and the Scholars Who Study Them* (Princeton, NJ: Princeton University Press, 2005), 198. For Orsi, this involves encounter and engagement with "lived religion" or the religious experiences and lives of others. This is a vastly different project of religious literacy than the one put forth here, which calls for not only an understanding of, but sharing and uniting with, those with whom one will be engaged. See also Orsi, *History and Presence* (Cambridge, MA: Harvard University Press, 2016); Loren D. Lybarger, "How Far is Too Far: Defining Self and Other in Religious Studies and Christian Missiology," *Journal of the American Academy of Religion* 84, no. 1 (March 2016): 127–56.

5. For discussion of these broader academic and cultural trends, see Perry L. Glanzer, Nathan F. Alleman, and Todd C. Ream, *Restoring the Soul of the University: Unifying Christian Higher Education in a Fragmented Age* (Downers Grove, IL: InterVarsity Press, 2017); *Christianity and the Soul of the University: Faith as a Foundation for Intellectual Community*, eds. Douglas V. Henry and Michael D. Beaty (Grand Rapids, MI: Baker Academic, 2006); James Tunstead Burtchaell, *The Dying of the Light: The Disengagement of Colleges and Universities from their Christian Churches* (Grand Rapids, MI: William B. Eerdmans Pub. Co., 1998); George M. Marsden, *The Soul of the American University: From Protestant Establishment to Established Non-Belief* (New York: Oxford University Press, 1994).

6. See also Douglas McConnell, "Evangelicals, Mission, and Multifaith Education" and Judith A. Berling, "What about Other Religions? Opportunities and Challenges in Mainline Theological Education," in *Disruption and Hope: Religious Traditions and the Future of Theological Education*, ed. Barbara G. Wheeler (Baylor University Press, 2019).

7. See also Matt Jenson, *Theology in the Democracy of the Dead: A Dialogue with a Living Tradition* (Grand Rapids, MI: Baker Academic Press, 2019), 80.

8. For further explanation of this turn toward critical literacy, see James Elmborg, "Critical Information Literacy: Implications for Instructional Practice," *Journal of Academic Librarianship* 32, no. 2 (2006): 192–9; Amanda L. Folk, "Reframing Information Literacy as Academic Cultural Capital: A Critical and Equity-Based Foundation for Practice, Assessment, and Scholarship," *College & Research Libraries* 80, no. 5 (2019): 1–27.

9. Mundelein Seminary has at times integrated its course in theological literacy, research, and writing with Master of Divinity courses in spiritual formation. It is

an approach that has generally been received positively by students and is a model I would advocate strongly for the reasons outlined above.

CHAPTER 2

Foundations for an Open Access Policy

ANDREW KECK, SOUTHERN METHODIST UNIVERSITY

O pen access (OA) is typically defined[1] as a framework for the online distribution of research that is "free" of cost and other barriers. While "open access policies" are a recent legal construct, some principles of open access are embedded in the past expressions of the Jewish and Christian theological traditions, including: oral stories and poetry, written narrative and laws, distributed letters and instructions, and tracts and books. These examples typically prioritized distribution to the widest possible audience while seeking to minimize costs and other barriers. A modern open access policy within a seminary or other institution of higher education attempts to make the scholarship of the institution (and particularly the faculty) freely available online to the widest possible audience. This chapter will address framing the faith and scholarly traditions that support an open access policy and accompanying digital repository, preparing the politics and process of adopting an open access policy, and implementing an open access policy within theological schools.

Sharing Faith: Faith Traditions and Open Access

In order to form faith across geography and time, the ancient Hebrews would retell stories through song and ritual, hold public meetings at the gate of the town, and read scrolls aloud. Over time, this led to the development and ongoing transmission of the biblical text. In an oral culture with a low level of literacy, the access challenge was primarily one of geography. In order to hear or (if literate) read from the texts, one simply had to be proximate to the texts and to those who could read.

A number of examples in the biblical text describe reading to those assembled. Famously, King Josiah is handed a scroll found during the renovation of the temple and "Then the king went up to the Lord's temple, together with all the people of Judah and all the citizens of Jerusalem, the priests and the prophets, and all the people, young and old alike. There the king read out loud all the words of the covenant scroll that had been found in the Lord's temple" (2 Kings 23:2, Common English Bible). Similarly, the scribe Ezra is ordered to read the law to "all the people gathered together" in Nehemiah 8. Likewise, Baruch reads the words dictated by Jeremiah in Jeremiah 36. Each reading is notably public and delivered to "all the people" without indication of an explicit admission fee to be present for those readings. There may indeed have been costs for being present, including costs for travel, the pause in labor, and taxes/tributes to be made, but there was no known extra charge for being a part of the hearing crowd.

The production and duplication of biblical texts was a costly enterprise in terms of the labor of a limited cadre of literate people and the basic elements of papyrus, scroll, etc. This work was compounded over decades, centuries, and millennia of transmission, revision, addition, and subtraction. These costs were largely borne by the cultic enterprise–either through a central authority or networks of cultic leaders and supporters.

Fast forward to the time of Jesus, who picked up the scroll of Isaiah and read to those gathered in the synagogue that day (Luke 4). Like the Hebrew Bible examples, there is no mention of payment for Jesus to borrow the scroll nor for the listeners to attend to his reading and teaching in the synagogue. Much of the corpus of the New Testament consists of letters that were widely distributed through extensive copying. Even the Apostle Paul indicates a collection of scrolls and parchments in 2 Timothy 4:13–the first Christian theological library.

While the funding and economics of copying texts is never directly addressed within the biblical text, the history of scribal copying and the development of the codex suggests that much of the duplication and transmission was centered around early scribal networks (Haines-Eitzen 2000). Manuscripts would travel through these scribal networks to be copied and combined with other manuscripts, often through a system of barter, gifts, and loans. Thus, new copies of manuscripts were created for and distributed to other scribes and to those with interests in propagating the faith. This is not unlike a precursor of open access–the journal exchange–where univerities publishing scholarly journals would exchange free subscriptions with other universities.

The advent of the printing press during the time of Martin Luther, and his own translation of the Bible into the German vernacular, increased the capacity to publish for wider distribution to a reading audience. Soon, a significant part of the spread of religious movements was directly related to the distribution of low-cost tracts and other materials to the largest possible population (Holborn 1942).

All of the examples above exhibit some barriers to "free." There's a geographic barrier to a public scroll reading in Jerusalem if you live in Jericho. To join in the retelling of stories or ritualistic actions, you need to know the language and/or have an allegiance to the tribe. While the Reformation's publishing practices certainly emphasized distribution, barriers included the actual cost, literacy, and the limited global distribution network. Even modern open access requires that readers overcome the potential barriers of internet access, tools enabling "discoverability," and digital literacy.

Open access does not mean there are no actual costs. The parchment must be bought, the scroll has to be written and copied, and the people must be gathered away from their work to listen. Reformation tracts also had to be written, printed, and distributed. An open access policy requires an institutional repository or other technological system to store and make these works available through a network and individual devices. Each of these has tangible costs and requires people with specific skills of writing, technology, and, increasingly, the law. To the degree possible, barriers and costs for the individual are reduced as much as possible and subsidized explicitly or implicitly by the cultic enterprise, government, wealthy patrons, and others. While the texts are known to be modified or selectively made available to support specific interests, a clear value remains within the tradition for providing religious instruction and texts to the widest possible audience.

Promoting Knowledge: Scholarship and Open Access

The analogy of an open access policy to the production/distribution of religious text has at least one significant difference from the work of a seminary or theological school: the work produced by most faculty tends not to be religious texts, but rather scholarship. Rather than strengthening existing faith and proselytizing others, scholarship advances an academic field of study. The impact of scholarship can also be directly related to its accessibility and distribution. If other scholars or practitioners related to an academic field of study do not have access to a work, they are unable to benefit from, critique, or further the scholarly insights.

Open access policies can be especially difficult to demystify and normalize due to the language of intellectual property, copyright, licensing, and mandates. For theological faculty, these can be unfamiliar and fraught terms within the relatively novel concept of open access and open access policies. In order for a faculty to approve an open access policy, they have to become more familiar and engaged with these concepts and terms. A more theological and historical framing (such as above) can often be a helpful starting place.

Legal issues cause many faculty to become uncomfortable, particularly in regards to navigating the significant relationships with their employing institutions and publishers. Faculty resist the idea of any institutional ownership of or encroachment upon their intellectual property. There can be a fear of an institution repackaging their content without permission, or in some egregious cases using (and thereby profiting from) a faculty member's intellectual property long after the faculty member has departed, retired, or died. Faculty can be nervous, in relation to publishers, about claiming too much in regards to their intellectual property, such that their current or future work might be ultimately rejected by the publisher. Faculty are more likely, as a result, to give away their copyright entirely and agree to unfavorable terms so that their works might be accepted for publication.

There has to be a level of understanding, comfort, and trust with the key idea of licensing intellectual property to others for an open access policy to be successful. Licensing is the key legal framework that makes open access work, moving from copyright law to contractual law.[2] Once understood and appropriately limited, licensing faculty intellectual property to one's institution and, when possible, to publishers, allows for maximum faculty ownership and flexibility in managing their own intellectual property.

Open access does not have nearly the uptake within humanities disciplines as in the sciences and social sciences. Theological faculty teaching or doing research in areas intersecting with the sciences or social sciences may have been more likely to have encountered open access. Thus, some basic description of open access may be helpful in order to provide the faculty with common baseline understanding. Ethical arguments could be made about engaging a global scholarly conversation or engaging practitioner scholars with limited resources. Also, open access is less known in the humanities/theology due not to the merits of the idea but to economics and the relative importance of journal and monograph publishing in the humanities. Humanities journals cost considerably less than science journals and the financial barrier for access to articles is not nearly as high, so the impetus and funding in the system for open access tends to be lower. Monographs tend to be more important in the theological disciplines, with business models for book publishing distinctive with more paid labor for acquisition, editing, design, and marketing.

Another argument is to demonstrate the growth over time of open access policies, particularly at the specific schools where faculty have received their doctoral degrees. The open access policies and accompanying repositories, in some cases, may be underutilized in the humanities/theology. But such a demonstration does help a faculty consider where their employing institution sits within the pantheon of theological schools dedicated to scholarship. It will also encourage the desire to participate in growing trends in scholarly communication.

The primary and determinative argument is about promoting access to faculty scholarship. Faculty tend to be particularly sympathetic to the idea of making their articles and essays available to a broader audience. In their own research, many have experienced wanting immediate access to an article in a journal or an essay in a book not available from the library. They could easily imagine the additional frustrations for global or isolated scholars and pastors who sometimes inquire directly to them for copies and offprints.

In preparing a Frequently Asked Questions or other document, librarians or other individuals promoting an open access policy need to position the policy as helpful and non-threatening. The policy reduces the need for individuals to negotiate with publishers. The policy positions the library to help faculty manage scholarly output and rights. One may need to emphasize that the seminary is not claiming or taking faculty copyright nor does this limit where faculty can publish. If there's a conflict, the institution will issue a waiver–no questions asked.

The open access policy itself can take any number of forms, but one of the most common is the Harvard Model Open Access Policy (*osc.hul.harvard.edu/modelpolicy/*). Anyone seeking to promote this to a faculty will need to become familiar with the specific language and reasoning behind each statement. Uninformed variations on the model can have unanticipated legal consequences. A faculty will want to tread carefully in attempting any edits. Some faculty, appropriately nervous to suggest changes to the text itself, may appreciate the opportunity to craft a longer preamble that articulates or theologically frames their own values and commitments. The Model Policy only states "The Faculty of XX is committed to disseminating the fruits of its research and scholarship as widely as possible." Most theological faculty could easily produce a more detailed rationale. Also, many local adoptions will dispense with the boilerplate references to "The Provost" or "Provost's Office" and simply indicate the appropriate named role within their own context.

Foundations for a Digital Repository

A digital repository, sometimes also referred to as an institutional repository (or IR), is an archive and mechanism for managing and storing the intellectual output of an institution in digital form. A digital repository can technically hold any digital object, but the focus on "intellectual output" tends to limit content to student dissertations, projects, or theses; faculty articles and other typically short-form works; institutionally-sponsored journals or magazines; and significant archival/historical materials produced by the institution. The key here is twofold. First, the repository is an archival collection based upon a connection to the institution itself and not as a disciplinary repository. Second, this organizing principle allows for an alignment with an institutional open access policy that is designed to collect and make available the scholarship produced by an institution.

Faculty experience with digital repositories may not be widespread. Some may have used or created profiles on service providers like academia.edu, or loaded materials to slideshare.net or figshare.com. Some younger faculty may have deposited their dissertations electronically within the institutions where they earned their doctorate. Even in R1 universities with active repositories and official open access policies in place, colleagues in schools of theology have less than a handful of faculty making regular deposits. If looking for support to approve an open access policy, faculty need to be able to see an active repository in order to seed their own imaginations.

One strategy is to begin to build and seed the repository with the publications of the most willing and politically influential faculty. Of course, open access policies tend to primarily address articles; when identifying initial faculty participants, one needs to identify faculty with the proper corpus of potential materials, as well as consider more carefully diversities of discipline, tenure, rank, gender, culture, and ethnicity. The idea is not to pre-build the entire repository but to seed it enough to provide some imagination to other faculty. Ideally, the faculty participating in this initial work will become important advocates, so it is important to make this as easy on faculty as possible—which means the library may be doing the bulk of the work. In many cases, one will have to work with the faculty member to provide pre-publication versions. Ideally, early adopters will also start to see hints of impact by seeing web analytics of others accessing their work, global queries of interest or appreciation, etc., which should make them ideal advocates.

Politics and Process of Adoption

Insightful arguments from the faith tradition and scholarly communication are insufficient to what is fundamentally a political process: the requirement of a faculty vote. Librarians, deans, and provosts forget this to their peril. Engaging the political process requires time and advocates. If one wants to successfully adopt and implement an open access policy, one must first start with the foundations. Can one argue theologically, ethically, and practically about open access and the potential impact of an open access policy? Can one develop enough of a proof-of-concept repository in order to provide faculty with vision of the process and impact? Has one learned enough about the issues around both repositories and open access policies to successfully advocate these to others, translating between legal/technical terms, theological values, and everyday language?

With these foundations in place, one must engage the proper process for approval. Some on nearly every faculty are sticklers for process and having appropriate time for deliberation and debate. If the open access policy is going to be part of the faculty handbook, then one will have to first engage with the committee with oversight of that handbook. Similarly, one may want to consult with the tenure and promotion committee and/or other committees devoted to faculty scholarship. Ideally, these smaller committees of the faculty create further circles of advocates for the open access policy. It can also be a place to test one's arguments and listen carefully for further concerns or objections. One can also ask for advice or recommendations in terms of what information, and in what format, might be most useful ahead of a faculty vote. Some might respond to an open forum; some might like to have a discussion at one meeting and hold off the faculty vote until the next.

If there are faculty who will voice strong objections, it is helpful to identify them sooner rather than later. One does well to listen carefully and acknowledge their concerns even if ultimately unable to persuade. In some cases, there may be faculty advocates willing to help intercede directly with their colleagues ahead of a general faculty discussion or meeting. At the faculty meeting itself, regardless of whether the vote is immediate, one can briefly lay out or recap the case for the open access policy and demonstrate the repository. Particularly among those already participating in the repository or other advocates, choose and prepare two or three to speak in favor.

Doing all the things noted above does not guarantee ultimate passage but does help maintain a positive tenor of faculty conversation. The ultimate goal is not simply the passage of a policy but development of a collective investment in and ownership of the policy. To implement the policy, one will largely be dependent on the faculty themselves to provide notification, appropriate versions, and metadata related to the production of new articles, essays, and other works appropriate to the open access policy and repository. A reluctant faculty vote may be a moral victory but, without a concomitant active participation, the implementation of the open access policy and growth of the repository will be limited.

Implementing an Open Access Policy

If one's faculty has passed an open access policy, congratulations! While the policy itself is effective for the present and future publications, one may want to continue to add prior faculty works as a means of building the content faster. Also, once individual faculty begin to see the impact of the repository and develop a comfort level with the process, active participation in the open access policy is encouraged.

A workflow can be organized depending on the size of faculty and available library staff (or other seminary staff) to deploy to this effort. To manage prior faculty works, one can use common bibliographic utilities (Atla Religion Database, OCLC WorldCat, Google Scholar) and faculty CVs to develop a comprehensive bibliography of faculty publications. Then, look up publisher copyright and self-archiving policies by using tools such as Sherpa Romeo (*sherpa.ac.uk/romeo/index.php*) that would allow posting the final published version. In many cases, one may need to ask individual faculty for pre-print versions of their articles. Don't forget that essays published within reference works and some other edited volumes can also be good candidates for inclusion. To add them to the repository, one will need to manage the actual files (usually PDF), develop standards for adding appropriate metadata and proper citation to the published work, and attend to other publisher requirements (typically embargos).

While the policy states that the faculty will submit articles, the reality involves implementing multiple approaches. Some faculty may indeed get into the habit of submitting appropriate articles to the digital repository with only a minimal need to check the quality of submission and metadata. Oftentimes, faculty will submit annual reports including lists of publications to the dean/provost or to staff in public affairs. If the open access policy can be integrated into these already-existing processes, it is more likely to become an institutional habit.

Conclusion

Two key factors are trust and normalization. By building the foundations with trust first and engaging in the faculty process, the result will be an approved and active open access policy that helps to feed the digital repository. The work of the open access policy and digital repository also needs to be normalized in two senses. First, positioning this work as "normal" in relation to historical precedents within the religious tradition, activities of other aspirational schools, and with a value for promoting faculty scholarship within a global environment. Second, this work must be normalized into institution workflows and faculty publication practices. While the effort can be difficult, a successfully implemented open access policy and digital repository can begin to have a significant virtuous cycle of increasing the scholarly profile and impact of a theological seminary.

Works Cited

Haines-Eitzen, Kim. 2000. *Guardians of Letters: Literacy, Power, and the Transmitters of Early Christian Literature.* Oxford: Oxford University Press.

Holborn, Louise Wilhelmine. 1942. "Printing and the Growth of a Protestant Movement in Germany from 1517 to 1524." *Church History* 11, no. 2 (June): 123–37.

Notes

1. For a broader overview, see Suber's *Open Access Overview* (*legacy.earlham.edu/~peters/fos/overview.htm*) or the Budapest Open Access Initiative (*www.budapestopenaccessinitiative.org/read*).
2. See especially the work of Creative Commons (*creativecommons.org/*) for further explanation and examples.

CHAPTER 3

Embracing the Future of Digital Libraries within Theological Libraries

PAUL A. TIPPEY, ASBURY THEOLOGICAL SEMINARY

*I*n 1938, H. G. Wells unveiled his vision of a "world brain," saying: "The time is close at hand when any student, in any part of the world, will be able to sit with his projector in his own study at his or her own convenience to examine any book, any document, in an exact replica" (1938, 77). In 1990, fifty-two years later, the first digital libraries began to appear. Although digital libraries are still evolving, the technical obstacles that dominated the first phase of digital library development have generally been overcome through advances in computers, networking, and algorithms (Lesk 2012). Universal access to "any book, any document" as envisioned by H. G. Wells is now both technically feasible and economically possible; however, significant social and legal barriers still remain.

In the coming years, digital theological libraries will provide access to a wide variety of resources, integrating content from diverse sources including images, texts, video, etc. These digital libraries will provide a seamless environment where research is transformed by the ability to filter, manipulate, and interact with materials like never before. Users of digital libraries will be both consumers and producers of information, both individually and in collaboration with others. With each of these changes, both past and future, the role played by libraries and information professionals must evolve. This chapter will examine the four principal barriers (technical, economic, legal, and social) to the development of digital theological libraries in order to prepare theological librarians for the challenges we face as we redefine the role of our profession in the days ahead.

Technical

H. G. Wells' 1938 vision set the stage for the development of the "world brain." In order for this to happen, the issue of machine translation, as well as that of information retrieval, had to be solved. In the 1960s, technical difficulties still existed at each stage of the process. The input stage consisted of keystroke documents in order to get the documents into a machine-readable form, a process that was vulnerable to input errors, the computation stage could only handle small collections, and the output stage was limited by retrieval systems. By the end of the 1960s, enough technology existed to build the first retrieval systems. With the establishment of computer typesetting and online access, commercial systems started to appear with Boolean search mechanisms. During the next two decades, essentially all production of published documents migrated to computers, and it became customary for a machine-readable copy of all new text to exist (digitally native content).

In the early 1990s, a breakthrough occurred that changed the future of digital libraries: algorithms for indexing and searching were created. Before this, the first internet-based searching-systems were based on manual indexing and hierarchical structures similar to traditional libraries. The advent of algorithm-based searching allowed large amounts of text to be inputted and every word to be indexed automatically. At the same time, professional scanners were available for publishers, print shops, and larger organizations to digitize traditional materials. This digitization process scanned the materials and saved them as images, and then optical character recognition (OCR) software was used to convert the image into an editable text with reasonable accuracy for searching capability.

In the 1990s, most people still preferred physical media. Screen reading was perceived as difficult and inconvenient, and people wanted the feel of paper and even the smell as they used the material (AntonBergen 2008 cleverly illustrates these attitudes). Even then, however, people were drawn to digital materials, as they could be instantly accessed from their desks and searched at the word level.

The popularity of digital materials grew as these advantages became better known. Perceptions really began to change when journals began to shift to digital format in the early 2000s. At first, most journals chose between paper or electronic versions; then they offered both versions. Now, twenty years later, some journals are shifting completely to electronic versions. Perceptions of digital books have also changed, particularly after the advent of the Amazon Kindle in 2007. By 2011, Amazon was selling more electronic books than physical books (Savitz 2011).

With the technological advances of the past several decades, technology has become less of a barrier to digital libraries. Technology has become less expensive, more reliable, quicker, and in some cases even automatic. The future is unknown, but with breakthroughs like Google's claims of "quantum supremacy," artificial intelligence could be the next breakthrough (Metz 2019), bringing us closer than ever to realizing Wells's vision of the "world brain."

Economic

It was unclear in the beginning, how this "world brain" was going to be economically supported. Many models have been used by commercial publishers such as monthly or yearly subscription fees, per-minute fees, access fees for signing up new users, transaction fees for downloading and advertising, and the cost charged per page. The per-minute and the access-for-signing-up-new-users models of sharing eventually collapsed. The per-minute model possibly collapsed due to the fact that plenty of people are willing to provide information for free, caring more about recognition than cash, or perhaps simply for the good of society. Regardless of the reason, the collapse of this early model of economic feasibility raises the question: how is this "world brain" going to be paid for (Lesk 2005, 597)?

Predominantly, the same sources that paid for information on paper are paying for it digitally: libraries, readers, and even authors and grants. Generally, publishers have converted paper publishing to electronic publishing to simplify their production process and, at the same time, increase their sales. Libraries (including theological libraries) have been using their acquisition budgets to purchase electronic copies in order to give users better services and avoid shelving costs. Meanwhile, individual readers can often buy current books on the Kindle or other electronic readers thanks to publisher programs. In addition, readers can buy individual articles if the library does not subscribe to the whole journal. Since electronic publishing can be done one copy at a time, self-publishing has been exploding for both books as well as scholarly articles.

Additionally, there has been a significant increase in open access options. When retrospective scanning is not provided by publishers and it falls within copyright laws to do so, many libraries will often do it themselves, sometimes funded by grants or donations, creating digital repositories of materials in their special collections. Some libraries have even established their own open access presses. [1]

The rapid spread of open access publishing is reshaping the very nature of academic publishing. In general, the funds needed for open access come from the authors, grants, donations, or library budgets. We do not yet understand whether a shift to open access will save theological libraries more in subscription fees than it costs them in repository operations. However, it is clear that an argument could be made that open access articles provided by students and faculty have a significant economic impact. In addition, open access articles are cited on average nine times while toll-access articles are cited on average six times, which can influence tenure and promotion decisions, affecting both individual faculty and institutions (Norris, Oppenheim, and Rowland 2008).

The change from print to digital resources may have been slow for theological libraries, but a great number of articles and books are available online today for free. Even more are available for purchase in a digital format. Clearly, economic problems continue to be a challenge for digital libraries, but, at the same time, the digital library is now economically possible.

Social

The largest issues facing the "world brain" are actually social in nature. Currently, the quantity of available material is outpacing the quality of the material. For example, the number of books being published is exploding, despite the fact that the number of books being sold is falling fast. Lesk (2012) asks, "How do we avoid a world in which junk information is taking over because the new world has less effective refereeing and reviewing?" Having access to more resources is good, but they need to also be usable resources.

A related issue has arisen through the use of the same search algorithms used to solve the technical problems explored above. Many algorithms are based on people's reviews and the number of downloads, but just because a resource is being used does not mean it is the best resource for a given situation. Additionally, when libraries use MARC records provided by a vendor or within some federated searching service, searches may inappropriately privilege that vendor's own resources. Furthermore, these third-party algorithms are owned by the company and generally cannot be seen or adjusted by the library. Additional issues arise because effective filtering tends to show people only what they agree with already.

Another social issue is the dependency of the "world brain" on private companies or non-profit organizations that rely on donors. Private companies have less of a responsibility to keep resources available; according to the website *Killed by Google* (www.killedbygoogle.com), for instance, Google has discontinued 194 different services to date. Although Google and other companies make some amazing resources available online, there is no guarantee those resources would survive the next dot-com crash. Similarly, non-profit organizations that rely on donors for survival could also be impacted in the long run by shifts in the cultural climate and their donors' shifting priorities.

According to Lesk (2012, 600) and based on sample study, large-scale book scanning projects like Project Gutenberg (est. 1971), the Million Book Project (est.

c. 2001), Google Books (est. 2004), the Open Content Alliance (est. 2005), and others have scanned pre-1920 US-published books more than six times (Lesk 2012, 598–99). While the rate of scanning has slowed, "this scanning project helped establish some important nodes in what's become an ever-expanding web of networked research" (Howard 2017).

This ever-expanding web of networked research nodes was helped by Google's scanning project. However, while Google was embroiled in decade-long litigation, the partner libraries wanted to make sure they kept their digital copies for research as well as for preservation. This desire led to the establishment of the HathiTrust Digital Library in 2008. The HathiTrust Digital Library contains more than 18 million monograph volumes, the majority coming from Google's scanning project (both public domain and copyrighted works), the Internet Archive, and local digitization efforts.

Another social shift for theological institutions is the significant changes to educational delivery methods which have influenced the growth of digital collections as well. Though the Association of Theological Schools initially had given specific guidance within the Educational Standards, prohibiting distance courses from constituting "a significant portion of a degree program," they seem to be backing away from this policy and have granted an exception to a number of schools, allowing for degrees offered completely online. To meet the needs of a growing population of distance learners, libraries must expand their access to digital materials through either purchase or digitization of printed materials.

Collaborative projects like HathiTrust could help solve most of these social issues. Quality control could be implemented that is similar to how MARC records were handled in the past or how Wikipedia uses crowdsourcing to sort materials and point readers to valuable, obscure materials. Additionally, companies should allow access to the algorithms or, at the very least, allow the library to have additional control of the algorithm. As for private companies and non-profit organizations, they should form a crowdsourced joint shared research node.

Legal

Despite the economic barriers to digital libraries being largely overcome, considerable legal barriers remain, particularly in the form of copyright law. Copyright law can be understood as an attempt to create an appropriate balance between competing interests. Copyright is not a natural right; it is a privilege granted by Congress, giving limited ownership of intellectual material to creators/authors. Initially, copyright was instituted to encourage the creation of creative works, but it has instead turned into a market place for financial enrichment (Lessig 2004, 6, 78). It is the foundational goal of copyright to enhance democratic culture and to support civil society as a whole. According to the US Constitution, the purpose of copyright is "To promote the Progress of Science and useful Arts, by securing for limited Times to Authors and Inventors the exclusive Right to their respective Writings and Discoveries" (art. 1, sec. 8, cl. 8).

Throughout history, copyright has adjusted to changing commercial practices and evolving technologies, e.g., lithography, radio, sculpture, cinema, television (both broadcast and cable), and reprography (U.S. Congress 1986). In 1976, Congress instituted copyright for the first time for unpublished manuscripts. Before 1976, creators/authors had to register a work with the Library of Congress and post a copyright notice on the work in order for the work to be protected under copyright. This is no longer the case. As soon as the creation is recorded on paper or some type of medium, it is now under copyright protection. In 1976, the United States Congress defined five exclusive rights possessed by copyright holders:

– to reproduce the work and to exclude others from reproducing;
– to derive new works from the work and to exclude others from making derivative works;
– to distribute copies and to exclude others from distribution copies;
– to perform the work–e.g., a play–publicly and to exclude others from so doing;
– to display the work–e.g., a poster–publicly and to exclude others from displaying it (*U.S. Code 17* [2006], § 106).

In the spring of 2003, the duration of this ownership was extended to the life of the creator/author plus seventy years for works not done for hire. On January 15, 2003, the *Sonny Bono Copyright Term Extension Act* was upheld by the United States Supreme Court (*Eldred v. Ashcroft*, 537 US 186).

Copyright law has directly impacted the rise of digital media and digital libraries, and it can be expected to continue to do so in the future. According to the ALA (2019), "Copyright issues are among the most hotly contested issues in the legal and legislative world; billions of dollars are at stake. Legal principles and technological capabilities are constantly challenging each other and every outcome can directly affect the future of libraries."

The development of the "world brain" does not align well with standard legal views about intellectual property. Traditionally, the author and/or the publisher were involved in the first-use market. The original purchaser had to buy the publication from a legitimate copyright holder. Once purchased, they could sell to a second-user market. This model assured that the author and/or publisher got their share of the profits from the initial sale, and it allowed the buyer rights to resell the item. Digital materials or items break down protections in both first-user and second-user markets.

Libraries and archives whose collections are open to the public have their own privileges and restrictions under copyright law, including the right to make copies of copyrighted works as long as there is no commercial advantage and the works are accompanied by a copyright notice. Three copies are allowed for preservation, but digital copies are not allowed outside of the library or archives. Under certain conditions specified in the copyright law of the United States (*U.S. Code* 17 [2006], § 108), libraries and archives are authorized to furnish a photocopy or other reproduction. One of these specific conditions is that the photocopy or reproduction is not to be "used for any purpose other than private study, scholarship, or research." In addition, the Fair Use provision in sections 106 and 106A allows for "...reproduction in copies or phonorecords or by any other means specified in that section, for purpose such as criticism, comment, news reporting, teaching (including multiple copies for classroom use), scholarship, or research" (*U.S. Code* 17 [2006], § 106–106A). If a user makes a request for, or later uses, a photocopy or reproduction for purposes in excess of "fair use," that user may be liable for copyright infringement. The institution must reserve the right to refuse to accept a copying order if, in its judgment, fulfillment of the order would involve a violation of copyright law.[2]

Fair use is vital to the growth of knowledge and can apply to a full range of materials and activities. Educational purpose alone does not automatically make a request fair use because each of the factors must be analyzed in order to conclude whether or not an activity is lawful. Fair use was designed by Congress to be flexible and adaptable to changing needs and circumstances. The law provides no clear and direct answers about the scope of fair use and its meaning in specific situations.

Despite this inherent flexibility, two specific 1980s court decisions concerning unpublished manuscripts have threatened the use of fair use. The first was the 1985 US Supreme Court ruling in *Harper & Row v. Nation Enterprises* (471 U.S. 539), which determined that the scope of fair use for unpublished materials is narrower than the scope for published works.[3] In 1987, even though traditional fair use allowed the right to quote from other materials specifically for purposes of research, scholarship, and education, the Second Circuit Court ruled in *Salinger v. Random House* that a creator/author could prohibit most uses of his unpublished letters even if deposited in archives. The court even excluded not only reprinting and quoting from the unpublished letters but also the detailed paraphrasing of the material. The court ruled that the original author who deposited their material in the archives only lost control of disposition, but retained full copyright of the material. This decision does not prevent donors from depositing papers within archives or archives from providing access to these materials, but it does affect how the archives' clientele can use the material.

For archivists, the challenge now is determining what is fair use. For unpublished manuscripts, fair use now depends not only on the four factors of fair use but also on the circumstances of the material in question. Privacy must now be taken into consideration along with copyright, even though they have directly conflicting purposes; while privacy laws want to protect confidential material, copyright seeks to promote the growth of knowledge. Archivists must adopt new strategies to control intellectual barriers in the aftermath of these recent changes.

As this brief overview shows, copyright law is a complex and ever-changing issue.[4] Because copyright applies to nearly every document, archivists and librarians need to be copyright leaders in their institutions, working to establish institution/organization-wide policies. These policies must include support and direction from librarians and archivists who are teaching and tutoring.

Institutional copyright policies must spell out two principles: first, all materials are generally under copyright, including unpublished materials, and second, there are some exceptions with fair use limitations. The policy must also identify specific responsible parties tasked with handling copyright for the institution or organization. These responsible parties must interact with legal counsel and must differentiate between professional association guidelines and actual law. Archivists and librarians must rely on law and not guidelines developed by organizations acting in their own organizational interests.

Institutional copyright policies must enumerate fair use privileges, asserting the full right of fair use allowed in each case. In order to accomplish this, policies need to be written to accommodate the grayness of copyright law, especially as regards fair use. In addition, the policy must include guidelines for seeking permission when fair use is not an option. There is no fast and easy answer for copyright; each case is different, and each case must be understood in its own context. For example, just because the ruling concerning unpublished material threw doubt/concern with fair use does not mean that it applies to every piece of unpublished material. Also, because of copyright expiration guidelines, the unpublished writings of authors will enter the public domain seventy years after death. These developments place another burden on archivists and librarians to record the deaths of writers represented in their collections.

In addition, when archivists or librarians obtain materials, they need to understand that they are not receiving the copyright of the material. Therefore, we must include a written form concerning copyright for all gifts and purchases, detailing the copyright provisions that will be in place upon the author's death. Archivists and librarians should then record this copyright ownership with the collection. Although, if copyright is not obtained with the collection, on the death of the author/creator the copyright may be equally divided and shared among multiple beneficiaries.

In the digital age, it is important to remember that every user is a creator and every creator is a user; therefore, it is imperative for libraries to be more than just gatekeepers of information. Librarians and archivists are called to help their clientele think critically, ask questions, foster creativity, and create (or simply foster re-creation of) information. We have a responsibility to protect and help clientele understand copyright. We have a duty to obey the law and to protect the agreed rights of the donors, but we also have a responsibility to make the collection as useful as possible for the clientele. Only by identifying and using fair use can we better fulfill both of these obligations.

For additional information and developments, please visit the following resources:

- *www.arl.org/copyright-timeline/*
- *www.copyright.gov*
- *www.librarycopyright.net*
- *www.copyrightoncampus.com*
- *www.copyright.com*
- *www.creativecommons.org/find/*
- *www.sxc.hu*

This section has described an unsolved problem for digital libraries–specifically, copyright law in the United States. Additionally, many issues of digital libraries will involve legal issues beyond copyright in the United States, such as international copyright laws, elaborate contracts, and technological protection software. Could you envision if there was a standard legal framework that was reasonable and straightforward to implement throughout the world?

Embracing the Future

Nearly a century after H. G. Wells unveiled his vision of a "world brain" in 1938, we are closer than ever to seeing that vision realized. Technological breakthroughs, combined with the social need for universal information access, have driven society to look for solutions to economic and legal barriers still facing digital libraries, spurring innovation and changes to copyright laws. There is still much work to do.

Digital libraries are transforming scholarship and research practices by increasing accessibility to materials that would otherwise not be accessible, by having no physical boundaries and providing around-the-clock availability, by allowing researchers and scholars to use any search term to investigate patterns in large amounts of text through friendly interfaces while increasing speed and accuracy of research, and by allowing print-disabled users to use technologies to read scanned books. In other words, digital libraries increase the preservation and conservation of resources while decreasing the physical space needed to store the same number of resources, as well as decreasing the cost of maintaining a digital library over a traditional library, and finally increasing the networking of resources across other digital libraries. Digital libraries have also spurred on innovation within the library, challenging librarians to learn new skills for learning, research, and creation. This has caused an increased focus on learning and development for digital learning, resulting in a shift from teaching and supporting information literacy face-to-face towards digital teaching and support. In digital libraries, innovation will also lead to even more advancements within data management, resulting in more accurate search results significantly improving the way researchers and scholars discover content.

This ever-expanding web of networked research nodes forms the "world brain" that Wells referred to in 1938. Digital libraries are a signature example of how research libraries have evolved beyond thinking of the isolated ivory tower. Expectations are shifting, and people want resources to be collectively held and available for all.

Innovations in digital libraries will, in turn, have an impact on the physical libraries. Clearly, there will be less public shelf space and more collaborative learning spaces, and the design of the library will be to better facilitate face-to-face interactions as well as digital learning interactions. This may require new, innovative technology that facilitates active learning spaces, media productions, virtual meeting spaces, etc. Additionally, partnerships with other areas of the institution (writing centers, instructional design, information technology, etc.) will need to be established to meet the needs of scholars and researchers. We can't be certain how the growth of digital material will manifest in the future; what is clear, however, is that digital libraries are changing the ways libraries are being used forever.

* * *

Disclaimer: I am not a lawyer and this should not be considered legal advice. You should seek appropriate counsel for your own situation. And please note, the section on legal challenges is directed toward readers in the United States. If you are conducting business outside the United States, I highly encourage you to find and understand your obligations regarding copyright and legal obligations for digital libraries.

Works Cited

AntonBergen. 2008. "Medieval Helpdesk in English." *YouTube*, February 23, 2008. *bit.ly/30lDne7*.

American Library Association. 2019. "Copyright for Libraries: General Information." Last updated March 21, 2019. *libguides.ala.org/copyright*.

Howard, Jennifer. 2017. "What Happened to Google's Effort to Scan Millions of University Library Books?" *EdSurge*, August 10, 2017. *bit.ly/2Th2xJv*.

Lesk, M. E. 2005. *Understanding Digital Libraries*. NewYork: Elsevier.

———. 2012. "A Personal History of Digital Libraries." *Library Hi Tech* 30: 592–603.

Lessig, Lawrence. 2004. *Free Culture: How Big Media Uses Technology and the Law to Lock Down Culture and Control Creativity*. New York: Penguin Press.

Metz, Cade. 2019. "Google Claims a Quantum Breakthrough That Could Change Computing." *New York Times*, October 23, 2019. *www.nytimes.com/2019/10/23/technology/quantum-computing-google.html*.

Norris, M., C. Oppenheim, and F. Rowland. 2008. "The Citation Advantage of Open-Access Articles." *Journal of American Society for Information Science and Technology* 59, no. 12: 1963–72.

Ogden, Cody. 2019. "Killed by Google." *killedbygoogle.com/*.

Savitz, Eric. 2011. "Amazon Says Now Selling More E-Books Than Print Books." *Forbes*, May 19, 2011. *bit.ly/2FQwcRW*.

US Congress, Office of Technology Assessment. 1986. *Intellectual Property Rights in an Age of Electronics and Information*. OTA-CIT–302. Washington DC: US Government Printing Office.

Wells, H. G. 1938. *World Brain*. Garden City, NY: Doubleday, Doran & Co.

Notes

1. For example, see *place.asburyseminary.edu/firstfruits/*.
2. For more information on fair use, please see *www.copyright.gov/fair-use/more-info.html*.
3. For additional information, see *supreme.justia.com/cases/federal/us/471/539/*.
4. For additional copyright development and information, see *www.arl.org/copyright-timeline/*.

CHAPTER 4

Topic Modeling as a Tool for Resource Discovery

SHAWN GOODWIN, ATLA, AND EVAN KUEHN, NORTH PARK UNIVERSITY

A s theological librarians look toward future developments in religious studies disciplines, many of the humanistic interpretive questions asked by researchers will remain the same. The biblical scholar will continue to explain the textual, philological, or ideological/theological coherence of biblical texts even as new methods for doing so are developed. Within systematic theology, the classic formula of *faith seeking understanding* articulated by Anselm of Canterbury has remained applicable in twentieth-century theologies and will remain a touchpoint in the future.

What will change, and what are currently in the process of immense change, are the methodological and technological aspects of theological research that allow us to ask and answer increasingly complex questions about sacred texts and religious communication. Although the digital humanities are sometimes (and often rightly) maligned by theologians as merely faddish, there are many examples of how computational methods are opening new possibilities for textual analysis, especially in biblical studies but also increasingly in theological research (see Anderson 2018; Robinson 2019). The fundamental problems of theology are not changed by digital methods, but the tools we have at our disposal for engaging in theological research have changed.

We are interested in investigating how digital humanities tools can address new problems of complexity within theology. In particular, we are interested in how topic models can be useful for determining new directions in theological research. In this paper, we will demonstrate how topic models can be used as a tool for resource discovery in emerging fields of study.

What Is a Topic Model?

Topic modeling is a statistical approach to grouping discrete collections of words based on similarity. The two dominant approaches used today are LDA (Latent Dirchlet Analysis) and NMF (Non-negative Matrix Factorization). "Topics" are groups of words that occur in proximity within a text. Each word is given a statistical weight that aligns with one of the topics.

Topics have often been used in digital humanities research to identify patterns in discourse for analysis (see Saxton n.d.). This work supplements the more traditional close reading approaches of literary and historical work by using computational methods of "reading," and is especially helpful for working with large bodies of texts. For example, Jeri Wieringa (2019) has used topic modeling to describe and visualize the relationship between end-times expectations and gender in early Seventh Day Adventist literature. Wieringa's research examined 31 periodicals spanning 77 years of publication, analyzing this literature at a depth that would not be possible with traditional methods of reading.

This is how topic models are typically used in digital humanities. In our case, we wanted to employ such models earlier in the process. If topic models are able to identify research-relevant patterns in texts, then could they also be used to recognize the research-relevance of texts for traditional (i.e., non-digital) modes of text analysis? To employ topic models in this way, we trained a topic model on a smaller, more recent, specific corpus that we selected for relevance using typical (i.e., keyword search) methods of discovery, and then used that model to filter works from a much larger historical corpus of political theology texts to identify any promising matches for the specific topics we were interested in.

Identifying New Knowledge in Theology

Resource discovery is often a solitary task, performed by theologians (or, if they are well-funded, by their research assistants) in preparation for a particular project. The description and organization of theological literature that makes discovery possible in the first place, however, involve a highly interconnected set of processes that are, in turn, sensitive to the changing nature of the research literature itself. When new constellations of research knowledge are produced, typical ways of describing research knowledge need to be adjusted. There can be a delay in learning what adjustments are most appropriate. There can also be an inability, because of various constraints, to go back to existing material and reorganize it in a way that might be more suitable under new circumstances. Soumenin and Toivannen (2016) have recently examined the helpfulness of

[handwritten marginal note:] ie watch filtering so the algorithms "do your research" for you on a large scale. You're at the mercy of tech accuracy – scanning/OCR + search result readings

unsupervised machine learning techniques for mapping new scientific knowledge in such situations, noting the inherent limitations of traditional descriptive metadata for identifying new constellations of scientific work:

> Preexisting categories of science provide a finite definition of new knowledge, fitting knowledge that is by definition infinite and new to the world into preexisting categories and coordinates[...] They are best at monitoring the behavior of known and defined bodies of knowledge, but lend themselves poorly–if at all–to correctly identifying the emergence of truly new epistemic bodies of knowledge. (Soumenin and Toivannen 2016, 2464)

Scientists working in physical, natural, and social scientific disciplines are well aware of the complex shifting ground upon which they work, and so computational approaches in these fields are already well established. Theology, along with other humanities disciplines, tends to lag behind in its embrace of digital humanities approaches. Where it does employ computational methods, it tends to use them for text mining, textual analysis, and visualization, rather than to map new knowledge.

Theological researchers often have much more traditionalist, even nostalgic, conceptions of their discipline and do not understand theology as a field in which emergent problems fundamentally change the nature of theological knowledge. For the good of the discipline, though, theological librarians need not grant that this problematic self-understanding of theological research is the case. They should investigate ways to most effectively engage with emerging constellations of theological problems so that new research is not overly restrained by descriptive schema that do not adequately map onto new theological questions.

New or dynamic fields of study present obvious challenges for mapping scientific knowledge, but they also present challenges for the researcher related to resource discovery of existing knowledge. Typical theological research is conducted with ready-made maps of knowledge available in the catalog and database metadata, but research in new fields may lack adequate descriptive metadata. Either the description of new texts is simply lacking, or it is inadequate because it does not capture new terminology or logical relationships that make these theological texts novel, much less connect these new relationships with older ones. In these situations, the theologian is left to map the new territory for themselves in an ad hoc fashion.

It is also difficult to identify which older texts might be applicable to the new theological situation, especially when new terminology is employed. For instance, searching a term like "Dreamer" (as in the DACA program) will not turn up any meaningfully related texts from the twentieth century, although there are surely older texts that communicate relevant concepts and ideas using different words. We propose that topic modelling is a tool that can help librarians and researchers alike as they tackle complex domains of new theological knowledge. Topic modelling can connect these domains with existing theological texts on the basis of patterns in these two otherwise discontinuous discourses.

We have focused this study on the emerging theological subfield of migration studies. Political discourse in the United States about the treatment of immigrants from Latin America, as well as the influx of refugees at a global level, most notably as a result of the Syrian Civil War, have made questions of migration and refugee identity an important, prominent, and growing subfield of political theology. As a result, terminology and research questions related to migration studies in theology are not as well established as more traditional fields such as christology, ecclesiology, or church history. For researchers conducting literature reviews and seeking out source material for the production of new knowledge in this and similar fields, it will be important to have discovery tools that are able to recognize and describe the relevance of sources in new and more complex ways.

(handwritten margin note: why is this the library's problem? the pt of researchers is to connect the dots + analyze them)

Topic Models for Resource Discovery: Theology and Migration

Creating the Model

First, we established a small corpus of known texts on theology and migration, from which we could derive topics that would guide our discovery of unknown texts in this subject area. We identified a small corpus of representative texts (monographs, edited volumes, and journal articles) published from 2010–19, using search keywords of [migration OR refugee OR immigrant] with [theology OR religion].[1]

Using PDFs of these texts, we created objects from the content with stop words removed (e.g., articles, commonly used words, etc.) and obvious misspellings and misdivided words fixed. We trained a model using the LDA (Latent Dirchlet Allocation) algorithm on these texts in order to generate topics that would be coherent but not have significant overlap. The visualization of these topics in figure 1 shows which words are most definitive of the topic and a visualized proximity of each topic to the others. This visualization also shows the dominance of particular words and the size of the topic in the entire corpus.

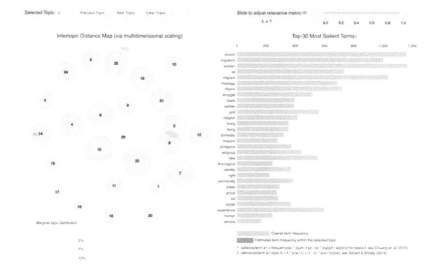

Figure 1

This figure shows a visual representation of the topic model we developed. An interactive version of this model can be viewed on *efkuehn.github.io/topicmodeldiscovery/docs/visualising_topic_model.html*.

One of the problems with topic modeling is that, because it is an unsupervised clustering method, sometimes the computer sees connections that are not obvious or, at the very least, are not *semantic* clusters. A topic model is a blunt tool, but we picked six of these topics that we thought might be helpful in discovering books over the past 100 years that might build on the topic we had chosen. We gave these topics headings in order to give them some sort of identifying description. The headings were derived from the word clusters as well as the pages that were best represented by these topics. We chose these topics because we thought they were coherent and might provide interesting analysis when looked at in the political theology corpus generated from HathiTrust.

These topics are:

– topic number: 0

- heading: Black Experience
- key terms: 'black, experience, life, mean, like, make, point, american, challenge, relation'

– topic number: 1

- heading: Context of Migrant Experience

- key terms: 'identity, challenge, term, experience, context, question, migrant, people, state'

- topic number: 3

  - heading: Communal Experience
  - key terms: 'migrant, country, home, community, family, experience, life, economic, new, reality'

- topic number: 5

  - heading: Social, Political, Economic Migrations
  - key terms: 'social, political, economic, immigrant, society, cultural, perspective, issue, people, life'

- topic number: 6

  - heading: Immigration and American Christianity
  - key terms: 'church, christian, american, immigrant, community, role, state, faith'

- topic number: 11

  - heading: Religion and Culture
  - key terms: 'religion, religious, culture, cultural, Christian, identity, faith, experience, example, time'

These are the only six topics we looked for in the HathiTrust corpus that we had identified. When using topic models for resource discovery, the researcher will need to make their own decision on what level of breadth or specificity will best fit the scope of their project.

Applying the Topic Model

The HathiTrust collection was created by searching for all works that might be related to Political Theology.[2] The collection on HathiTrust was further filtered by matching the OCLC numbers with connection to pull out valid subject headings. This left a series of about 9,000 books. These books were further filtered to exclude any that did not have an English language tag. The final count of HathiTrust books we gathered was 6,260. One of the limitations of the topic model we are using is that it can only be used for a single language. Although some work has been done on topic models in multilingual contexts, this is an area where the digital humanities will need to improve upon current options.[3]

Distribution of Topics

We grouped the records by decade and then proceeded to count all of the pages that were dominated by the specific topics. Sorting the data this way gives a nice overview of the corpus (figure 2). These counts correspond to the amount of materials we had from each year. It also shows that Topic 5 is the most common in this corpus. When we went back and looked at the keywords for this topics, it became clear why these words showed up so commonly. Many of these books aren't necessarily about migration exactly, but society, politics, and economics are covered thoroughly in many of the books in our corpus.

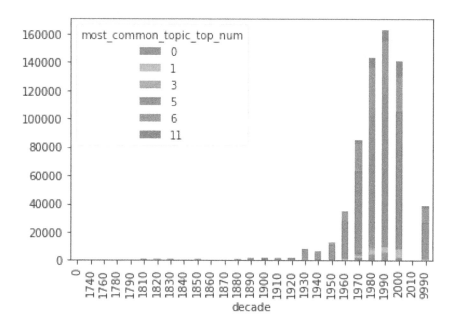

Figure 2

Topic Average Distribution

We also averaged the topic fit percentage across the corpus for each decade. One interesting aspect of this chart (figure 3) is the decades that don't include any instances of one or more of the topics. It would be worth investigating further if this is just a weakness in our corpus or if it reflects a trend in the period.

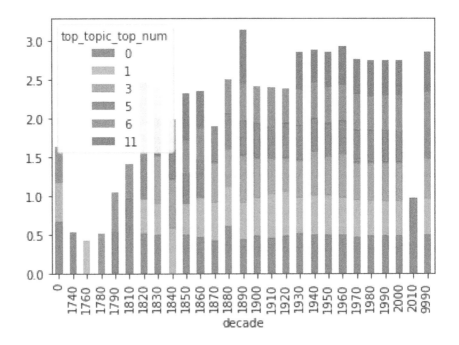

Figure 3

Using the Topics For Discovery

We filtered the topic matches based on which pages had the greatest percentage of a match, as well as having the most pages that had that topic as the dominant topic. These topics produced a lot of noise, but in that noise many interesting potential books also appeared in the results. The following books seem to relate well or suggest interesting, if non-obvious, connections with our area of study:

– Topic 0: Black Experience

- *Selected Black American, African, and Caribbean Authors: A Bio-bibliography* / compiled by James A. Page and Jae Min Roh. 1985.

> *Subjects:* Authors, Black Biography Dictionaries. | Caribbean literature Black authors Bio-bibliography. | African literature Bio-Bibliography. | African American authors Biography Dictionaries. | American literature African American authors Bio-bibliography.

- *Afro-American Life, History and Culture* / developed for USIS Programs by the Collections Development Branch, Library Programs Division, Office of Cultural Centers and Resources, Bureau of Educational and Cultural Affairs, United States Information Agency. 1985.

  > *Subjects:* African Americans Social conditions Bibliography. | African Americans Bibliography.

– Topic 1: Context of Migrant Experience

  - *Who's Who in American Jewry*, v. 3, 1938–1939. 1939.

  > *Subjects:* Jews Biography Periodicals. | Jews United States Biography Periodicals.

  - *Joy of the Worm* / Sargeson, Frank. 1969. [4]

– Topic 5: Social, Political, Economic Migration

  - *The Blackwell Companion to Globalization* / edited by George Ritzer. 2007.

  > *Subjects:* Internationalisation | Globalization.

  - *Social Aspects of Alienation: An Annotated Bibliography* / Mary H. Lystad. 1969.

  > *Subjects:* Social Problems abstracts. | Social Isolation abstracts. | Alienation (Social psychology) Bibliography.

  - *Bystanders to the Holocaust* / edited with an introduction by Michael R. Marrus, v. 3. 1989.

  > *Subjects:* Jews United States Politics and government. | Jews Palestine Politics and government. | Jewish refugees. | Holocaust, Jewish (1939–1945) Public opinion.

– Topic 6: Immigration and American Christianity

  - *The Indian Church* / Virag Pachpore. 2001.

  > *Subjects:* Christianity India.

- *Dalits in India: Religion as a Source of Bondage or Liberation with Special Reference to Christians* / James Massey. 1995.

  > *Subjects:* Dalits India Religion. | Discrimination India. | Caste India. | Christians India.

- *An Introduction to the Reformed Tradition: A Way of Being the Christian community* / John H. Leith. 1977.

  > *Subjects:* Reformed Church Doctrines

– Topic 11: Religion and Culture

  - *The Enlightenment, An Interpretation: The Rise of Modern Paganism* / Gay, Peter (1923–). 1966.

    > *Subjects:* Philosophy History. | Enlightenment. | Europe Intellectual life.

  - *Predicting Religion: Christian, Secular, and Alternative Futures* / edited by Grace Davie, Paul Heelas, Linda Woodhead. 2003.

    > *Subjects:* Twenty-first century Forecasts. | Christianity Forecasting. | Religion Forecasting.

  - *Ernst Troeltsch and the Future of Theology* / edited by John Powell Clayton. 1976.

    > *Subjects:* Troeltsch, Ernst, 1865–1923 Congresses.

Applications

This project demonstrated the potential usefulness of topic modeling for exploring a larger corpus and for providing a supplement to traditional library metadata. However, it also illustrates some challenges to be aware of. The parameters of a topic model can vastly improve its ability to provide helpful results for research. Two parameters that we should have improved on are the filter extremes and the number of topics. Filter extremes are a type of limiter for a model, functioning in a similar manner to stop words. The researcher can set filter extremes to cut out any words that do not occur in very many documents, or on the other hand to cut out words that occur in most or all of the documents. Each of these cut-offs is simply a predetermined numerical value. This can help the model from relying too much on the extremes of language use. However, because we built our model on such a small corpus and then applied it to a much larger, historical corpus, the extremes of our training set may have actually been part of what we were looking for. In light of this difficulty, another way of improving this study would be to more carefully curate both the training set and the larger corpus explored using the topic model. Many of the works in this larger corpus have little or nothing to do with theology, and we should remove some of them. In addition, our training corpus could have been more carefully selected around a specific topic and made larger. Both of these steps could vastly improve the results of our experiment.

A further step could be to filter the larger HathiTrust corpus on a constellation of topics. We could use two or three topics that create an interesting look at a topic. One way this could work is to train the topic model so that migration and theology are distinct and coherent topics, and look for a work that has a predominance of both of those topics. If we were to do this, we would need to record more than just the top-ranked topic for a document, but also the second and third as well. This approach would also be a promising way to build on our current project by focusing the scope of the topics used.

JSTOR's Text Analyzer also uses a topic model to match uploaded papers to additionally interesting ones.[5] However, JSTOR's method is nearly the reverse of ours: JSTOR starts with their large corpus, and then tries to fit the new paper into the model. Instead, we start with a smaller data set and try to filter things out. JSTOR's approach is a more traditional use for topic modeling. However, there are other algorithms for matching texts that might provide better approaches for discovery. Algorithms like Google's PageRank algorithm could also be leveraged for digital humanities projects like ours.[6]

Work has also been done on using topic models for query expansion, and our own project can be understood in terms of query expansion, insofar as our initial selection of a text corpus for training our topic model was an initial query, which we then expanded for use in further resource discovery (see Yi and Allen 2009). Some of the strategies mentioned above for curating the data set, as well as constraining the model, will help in guiding the task of query expansion.

One benefit of using topic modelling for resource discovery, in contrast to more typical uses of topic models in digital humanities, is what can be called the "low stakes" of this use. Bernard Schmidt (2012) has offered caution about the helpfulness of topic models for discovering conceptual patterns in text corpora, point out that, "excitement about the use of topic models for discovery needs to be tempered with skepticism about how often the unexpected juxtapositions LDA creates will be helpful, and how often merely surprising. A poorly supervised machine learning algorithm is like a bad research assistant. It might produce some unexpected constellations that show flickers of deeper truths; but it will also produce tedious, inexplicable, or misleading results." At the stage of resource discovery (rather than "discovery" within textual analysis itself), this possibility of merely apparent pattern recognition is still present. That said, a researcher who is going through an initial selection of relevant sources is not performing textual analysis, but rather is merely identifying texts using analysis of topics as a preliminary way to judge relevance. This use of topic modelling will rarely, if ever, be paired with a topic model's typical use of text analysis later on in the research project, since a corpus of texts determined at such a level of specificity at the stage of resource discovery will be too small and selective to be used for genuine analysis using topic models. Recall from some of the examples above, topic models in the digital humanities usually examine long runs of periodicals or large amounts of longitudinal data, rather than bibliographies of works preselected as relevant to a particular research project.

The low stakes of resource discovery do not give the researcher license to use topic modeling without proper care, however. Resource discovery is "high stakes" in its own ways. It takes time to teach an algorithm how to function properly and time for it to process large amounts of literature. When texts are identified using topic models, a false positive may not lead to faulty analysis in published research; more likely it will be recognized as irrelevant and discarded. But this time wasted working with irrelevant texts that do not help the research process is a real cost of topic modeling for resource discovery. Whether such wrong turns and wasted time are any more present using this method than they are in resource discovery using subject authorities or single keyword searches is an open question. But this is a cost of which researchers should be cognizant.

Topic modeling for resource discovery is a tool that should be used when the significance of the research project warrants such measures. It is also a tool that should be further developed by information specialists and even formally incorporated into library or database discovery layers. Ideally, theologians who are open to digital humanities methodologies and theological librarians who are equipped to engage at a deeper level with the content of emerging fields of study will work together to improve upon these and other new tools for theological research.

I really don't see how this is different from keyword searches too much

Works Cited

Anderson, Clifford. 2018. "Digital Humanities and the Future of Theology: What Potential Does Digital Humanities have to Shape the Practice of Theology? Are There Theological Questions at Stake?" *Cursor: Zeitschrift für explorative*

Theologie, 25 July 2018. *cursor.pubpub.org/pub/anderson-digitalhumanities–2018*.

Kuehn, Evan and Shawn Goodwin. 2018. "Indexing the Theologico-Political." *Atla Summary of Proceedings* 72: 168–72. *doi.org/10.31046/proceedings.2018.129*

Robinson, Matthew Ryan. 2019. "Embedded, Not Plugged-In: Digital Humanities and Fair Participation in Systematic Theological Research." *Open Theology* 5, no. 1: 66–79. *doi.org/10.1515/opth-2019-0005*.

Saxton, Micah. n.d. *Best Practices for Topic Modelling*. Accessed July 8, 2020. *msaxton.github.io/topic-model-best-practices/*.

Schmidt, Benjamin. 2012. "Words Alone: Dismantling Topic Models in the Humanities." *Journal of Digital Humanities* 2, no. 1. *journalofdigitalhumanities.org/2-1/words-alone-by-benjamin-m-schmidt/*.

Suominen, Arho and Hannes Toivanen. 2016. "Map of Science with Topic Modeling: Comparison of Unsupervised Learning and Human-Assigned Subject Classification." *Journal of the Association for Information Science and Technology* 67, no. 10: 2464–76.

Vulić, Ivan, Wim de Smet, Jie Tang, and Marie-Francine Moens. 2015. "Probabilistic Topic Modeling in Multilingual Settings: An Overview of Its Methodology and Applications." *Information Processing & Management* 51, no. 1: 111–47. *doi.org/10.1016/j.ipm.2014.08.003*.

Wieringa, Jeri E. 2019. "A Gospel of Health and Salvation: Modeling the Religious Culture of Seventh-day Adventism, 1843–1920." PhD diss. George Mason University. *dissertation.jeriwieringa.com/*.

Yi, Xing and James Allen. 2009. "A Comparative Study of Utilizing Topic Models for Information Retrieval." *Proceedings of the European Conference on Information Retrieval* 5478: 29–41.

Notes

1. The full project site for Topic Modeling as a Tool for Resource Discovery is available at *efkuehn.github.io/topicmodeldiscovery/*. The bibliography for the textual corpus is available at *docs.google.com/document/d/1sXHkN6WsW_SwG5xLSRPLS-DPqbwbQCHcB8ErrIbxu0M/edit?usp=sharing*.

2. The HathiTrust collection can be viewed here: *babel.hathitrust.org/cgi/mb?a=listis&c=1154484*. This collection was originally created for Evan Kuehn and Shawn Goodwin, "Indexing the Theologico-Political," *Atla Summary of Proceedings* 72 (2018): 168–72, *doi.org/10.31046/proceedings.2018.129*.

3. Some work has been done on multilingual models. For example, this model creates a bilingual LDA model: Ivan Vulić et al., "Probabilistic Topic Modeling in Multilingual Settings: An Overview of Its Methodology and Applications," *Information Processing & Management* 51, no. 1 (January 1, 2015): 111–47, *doi.org/10.1016/j.ipm.2014.08.003*. In general, more work needs to be done in multilingual and low-resource language natural language processing techniques.

4. This is a novel that does not have any fulltext available in HathiTrust, or for that matter any description readily available online. The source itself may not end up being helpful, but it is interesting insofar as it is the sort of text that a typical search for migration-related literature would not turn up.

5. See JSTOR Labs, *Test Analyzer: About*, *www.jstor.org/analyze/about*.

6. For example, see this implementation in Python: *github.com/ashkonf/PageRank*.

CHAPTER 5

Current Trends in Religious Studies & Theology Collection Development

MEGAN E. WELSH AND ALEXANDER LUIS ODICINO, UNIVERSITY OF COLORADO (CU) BOULDER

C ollection development facilitates patron access to information, a core value of librarianship. It is a way in which the profession empowers patrons in critical thinking and knowledge creation. Without relevant materials that meet the needs and challenge the minds of library users, librarians are not optimizing patrons' ability "to become lifelong learners–informed, literate, educated, and culturally enriched" (American Library Association 1999).

This chapter encourages the theology or religious studies librarian to think deliberately about the needs of their patrons and about strategies to develop an enriching collection that meets these needs. Results from a recent study describe the current collection development trends in the discipline.

Literature Review

Research relating to religious studies and theology collection development can be categorized into two areas: identifying patron information needs and describing methods for engaging in collection development activities.

In the recently published second edition of Gregory's (2019) *Collection Development and Management for 21st Century Library Collections*, the author encourages librarians to frame collection development through an assessment of user needs, stating, "Knowledge of the community that the library serves... is the keystone of effective collection development" (13). On a local level, Gregory suggests approaching a needs assessment periodically (as patrons and their needs change) and preparing for this assessment by asking questions: who and what will be studied?; where are data collected?; when should the data be collected?; and how are the data interpreted? (14–18).

On a disciplinary level, a recent study sponsored by Ithaka S+R explores the information needs and practices of religious studies and theology scholars (Cooper et al. 2017). This research, conducted across 18 institutions of higher education, concluded that "digital discovery and access have greatly improved these scholars' research experiences with relatively few challenges" (15), though scholars do face barriers to incorporating digital methodologies (such as digital humanities) into their research. Other researchers, such as Knievel and Kellsey (2005), who conducted a citation analysis across humanities fields, and Shirkey (2011), who conducted a syllabus analysis "to really understand what students go through" (159), can complement Cooper et al. (2017) by providing another perspective into information needs of religious studies scholars and students. Knievel and Kellsey's (2005) study found that 88.2% of citations in their sample of religious studies scholarship were of monographs. This was the highest of the eight humanities fields they investigated and reaffirms Hook's (1991, 216) statement that "religious and theological discourse continues to rely more heavily on book length monographs." While Cooper et al. did not focus on the format of information that scholars consumed, they did note that scholars reported analyzing "primary and secondary source material in both physical and digital forms" (2017, 20). Since this research found that digital availability of secondary sources supports religious studies scholarship, librarians may be motivated to consider purchasing more digital monographs in e-book format. Understanding evolving information needs and research practices can help religious studies and theology librarians to purchase materials that meet the needs of patrons in these disciplines.

Several works emphasize the importance of personally engaging with patrons in order to identify their needs (Alt 1991; Gregory 2019; Little 2013; Schmersal, Dyk, and McMahan 2018). Strategies include speaking with faculty and students (especially graduate students) (Alt 1991; Schmersal, Dyk, and McMahan 2018) and consulting members of the curriculum committee to gauge needs with the understanding that collection development decisions "cannot be made in a vacuum" (Alt 1991, 209). Alt goes on to describe the importance of using both "collection-centered" and "client-centered" methods to determine patron needs. Where collection-centered collection development methods seek to compare the library to that of a peer institution, client-centered methods mean conducting surveys and interviews to determine the present strengths and weaknesses of the collection in meeting user needs (211). Alt's article and its implications for collection development activities can be updated and expanded upon, especially by engaging with librarians who currently track patron needs and research trends and who purchase materials in this modern information landscape.

In a presentation at Atla Annual, Schmersal, van Dyk, and McMahan (2018) outlined the importance of keeping abreast with research trends. They described methods for staying current that ultimately inform collection development practices and meet the needs of their patrons. Van Dyk, through a survey to Atla members via a listserv commonly used by religious studies and theology librarians, found that professional colleagues, academic conferences, and academic journals were the most common ways that librarians kept current with trends in the discipline (143). Through interviews with two graduate students, Schmersal also found that conferences, journals, and peer work, especially expressed via social media, are ways that graduate students monitor research trends. Of most importance to the graduate students with whom Schmersal spoke were filling gaps in journal series, accessing digital tools (such as Omeka), and acquiring materials representing the interdisciplinarity of their work (146). In a field which "is both difficult to define and impossible to categorize neatly or easily" (Alt 1991, 208), library users and librarians have echoed the necessity and challenges of building a comprehensive collection based on the interdisciplinary nature of religion and theology (Alt 1991; Hook 1991, 216; Cooper et al. 2017). Beyond the studies named here, more research should be conducted to identify how religious studies and theology librarians are meeting disciplinary information needs through collection development activities.

Methods of Collection Development

A variety of suggested techniques for developing a collection emerge from literature spanning decades. Many of the techniques published in older texts are still relevant to today's librarian. A special issue of "Library acquisitions: Practice and theory" from 1991, which focused on religion and theology collection development, outlined collection development practices such as creating and using a collection development policy to guide purchasing decisions (Alt 1991), considering the level of financial support in determining the scope of the collection

(Alt 1991; Hook 1991), consulting sources that provide book reviews (e.g., *Choice*), and turning to others, including comparing catalogs at other peer institutions and consulting professional organizations where association publications and individual colleagues may provide recommendations about which titles to purchase (Alt 1991). While Hook (1991) broadly had negative experiences with approval plans in a theological library context, Alt (1991, 212) cites approval plans as a good way to "receive many titles automatically." Hook communicates the enormity of the task of selecting and purchasing materials and how overwhelming collection development can be without effective automated mechanisms for acquiring new titles. He states that "[t]he prospect for reviewing the multitudes of publishers' catalogs, advertisements, professional journals, and so forth for newly published titles in religion is a daunting one" (Hook 1991, 216). Yet this remains a common strategy for librarians and, indeed, Alt (1991) recommends reviewing publisher's catalogs, especially those associated with a specific geographic or denominational perspective. Seemingly timeless, reviewing publisher catalogs, vendor services, book reviews, and other sources (especially websites) that curate lists of recommended titles is a suggested method treated by Gregory (2019) in chapters entitled "Selection Sources and Processes" and "Acquisitions." Additionally, the importance of creating collection development policies, "which serve as blueprints" and support the library in "acquiring, organizing, and managing library materials" (Gregory 2019, 29), is echoed beyond this special issue from 1991 throughout the literature, including in two book chapters focused on special collections and archival and manuscript collecting in a volume commemorating Atla's 50th anniversary (Graham et al. 1996) and, most recently, in a full chapter in the second edition of Gregory's (2019) *Collection Development and Management for 21st Century Library Collections.*

Little (2013) encourages readers to consider collection development in ways that align with the Association of Theological Schools' (ATS) accreditation standards. In a book chapter that provides a comprehensive overview of how librarians, especially early-career librarians, can build collections that support theology graduate school programs–a very specific setting and patron population– Little (2013, 113) emphasizes the importance of the accreditation, stating that "those seeking to be ordained... must hold a degree from an institution accredited by the" ATS. The ATS's *Standards of Accreditation* centers teaching and learning around the library and states that "[t]he library is a central resource for theological scholarship and education" (ATS Commission on Accrediting 2015, 10). The preeminent accrediting body of the theological field indicates that the library and its collection are of critical importance to the intellectual formation and professional success of theological school graduates. Little (2013, 113) suggests that, regardless of level of experience, librarians should refer to the *Standards of*

Accreditation as a resource to inform their collection development practices. The primary audience for this book chapter seems to be librarians who are new to the field and to collection development responsibilities. Little addresses the evolution of formats of materials relevant to the field, acknowledging that, currently, the accessibility of materials in an electronic format is commonplace (115). The chapter provides a valuable introduction to theological resources. Little names specific resources that would be valuable to the collection and describes the variety of formats (e.g., print materials, e-books, CD-ROMs, etc.), the diverse nature of content types (e.g., concordances, dictionaries, Biblical commentaries, etc.), and the nature of the content (e.g., sacred texts, scholarly secondary resources) that should be included in a theological library. In the context of subscribing to journals, and arguably for the acquisition of any library material, Little states that "the librarian must always have the program's curriculum in mind, as well as current specializations within the curriculum or historical collecting and research interests" (120). Although many of these materials and strategies are also applicable in a secular religious studies library, some, such as collecting texts about church administration and ensuring a breadth of materials from a specific Christian denomination, would be less relevant in this context. The strategies Little mentions are especially helpful for those developing a collection in an institution affiliated with or focused on Christianity. Beyond Christianity, Little does include a paragraph about other faith traditions, citing ATS standards requiring accredited libraries to include "basic texts from other religious traditions" (ATS Commission on Accrediting 2015, 10), whereas a secular library or a library serving a religious studies program would have not only these basic texts but a larger collection of texts related to each religious tradition.

In addition to the more traditional methods already discussed, a few stood out as more creative and appropriate for the current information landscape. Shirkey (2011) collected 98 syllabi from a variety of humanities fields, including religion, and framed the study as a user-centered method that can "generate items for inclusion in the library's collection" (157), ultimately benefiting "the collection, the librarian, and the library as a whole" (154). At the time of writing, Shirkey could only identify three other studies that used syllabi as an aspect of collection development. This case study demonstrated that 68% of the 936 required or supplementary texts were held in the library, indicating that librarians responsible for purchasing materials could review syllabi to be more aware of core course-related needs and order titles to fill these needs. McMahan (2018) emphasized the importance of social media as a way for librarians to stay current in the field. She described social media as "a promising avenue for discovering new publications and emerging trends in a given area of research," focusing specifically on using social media as a tool "to find resources to build collections in a new research area" (147). Included in this presentation were extensive lists of scholars to follow on Twitter and links to podcasts, blogs, and more that would help new and experienced librarians alike to gain ideas for resources to add to their collections.

Identifying Current Collection Development Trends

As described, there are a variety of ways through which librarians engage in collection development activities, all while balancing purchasing priorities and patron needs. This section describes a study conducted in December 2019–January 2020 and discusses broader trends in the current religious studies and theology collection development landscape.

Research Questions

The purpose of the study is to explore how library professionals responsible for acquiring materials related to the fields of religious studies and theology at institutions of higher education in the United States and Canada engage in collection development activities. The researchers posed the following questions:

– What methods do religious studies and theology librarians use to purchase library materials?
– What are religious studies and theology collection development trends in the United States and Canada?

To answer these questions, the researchers developed a survey to send to librarians responsible for collecting in these disciplines.

Recruitment & Respondents

In fall 2019, the researchers developed a list of librarians employed at 114 public and private academic Association of Research Libraries (ARL) member libraries presumed to have collection development responsibilities for the disciplines of religious studies or theology. At times, we listed multiple individuals from the same institution, especially if one was listed as a subject specialist for religious studies and another as a subject specialist for Judaism, for example. Of the 114 ARL institutions, we could not find information for a religious studies-related librarian at nine institutions. Across the remaining 105 institutions, and accounting for multiple librarians who may have religion- or theology-related collection development responsibilities, our total list consisted of 142 ARL librarians. The researchers emailed a survey (see appendix) in December 2019 to these ARL librarians and, in January 2020, to the 595 members subscribing to the Atlantis listserv (T. Burgess, pers. comm., January 10, 2020)–a listserv used by religious studies and theology librarians who are not necessarily employed at ARL institutions. Recipients were invited to forward the recruitment email with a link to the survey to others within their institution who may be more well-suited to respond to collection development practices in religious studies and theology. This methodology means that we are unsure of the exact number of recipients with access to the survey.

The survey was open for 3.5 weeks and one reminder email was sent to the list of ARL librarians and to the Atlantis listserv. A total of 86 librarians who clicked the survey link and who were eligible completed the survey. Seven additional librarians began the survey, but were deemed ineligible and filtered out based on the first two questions which asked respondents to confirm that they are responsible for collection development to support the study of religion or theology at their institution and that their institution is located in the United States or Canada.

Respondents answered a maximum of 22 survey questions, including multiple choice, rank order, and open text box questions that provided rich contextual information. Some questions were only made visible to some respondents based on previous responses, and the researchers decided not to require respondents to answer any of the questions except the first two, which determined eligibility.

Of the 78 respondents who answered the question "At what stage are you in your career?" the majority of respondents (37.2%, n = 29) identified themselves as mid-career (see figure 1). A significant number of respondents are experienced librarians, with half of all respondents (48.8%, n = 39) identifying themselves as either advanced career librarians (23.1%, n = 18) or nearing retirement (26.9%, n = 21).

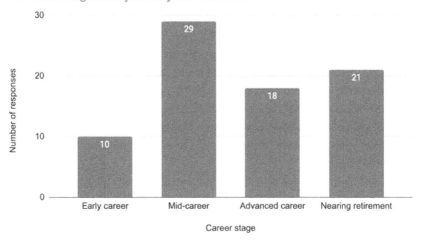

At what stage are you in your career?

Number of responses

Career stage

Figure 1: Represents the results of question 15.

A slight majority of 78 respondents identified their institutional affiliation as a public university or college (28.2%, n = 22) while 21 respondents (26.9%) identified that they are employed at a stand-alone seminary (see figure 2). While we did not ask respondents to identify the name of their institution or whether or not it is an ARL member library, these responses may indicate a good distribution of participation from librarians at both ARL libraries and those recruited from the Atlantis listserv. We acknowledge that one's institutional affiliation may look different from the options we provided, so we allowed respondents to tell us about their institutional affiliation in an open text field. The majority of the six people who chose "other" indicated that their institution was a combination of the options we offered. We also offered respondents the opportunity to report if their institution is affiliated with a specific religious tradition and denomination, and 44 respondents identified their institution's affiliations using an open text box. The researchers coded 42 of these as Christian and two respondents specifically identified their institutions as "inter-religious."

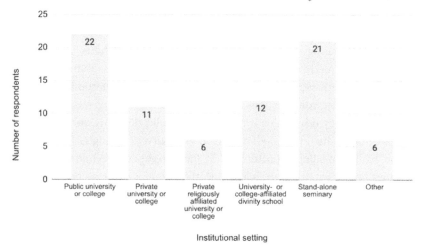

Please choose the answer that best describes your institution.

Figure 2: Represents the results of question 16.

Additionally, we wanted to gather information about the nature of religious studies and theological programs at their institutions and the student body with whom the respondents work. Most institutions (32.5%, n = 26) reported a total institutional enrollment (including undergraduates and graduates) of less than 1,000 students. Interestingly, the next most popular responses represented institutions at very different ends of the size spectrum: thirteen respondents (16.3%) reported that their school has between 1,001 and 5,000 students, and twelve respondents (15%) reported that their school has more than 35,000 students. It is important to note that the majority of respondents (58.8%, n = 47) come from schools with a total enrollment of 10,000 students or less.

More respondents (66) reported on the number of graduate students seeking degrees in religious studies or theology than those who shared the number of undergraduates seeking degrees (54 respondents). The majority of respondents (35.2%, n = 19) indicated that the number of undergraduate students seeking degrees in religious studies or theology is less than 25 students. Looking at those who reported that their institution grants graduate degrees, the majority (50%, n = 33) indicated that they have over 100 students seeking these degrees. In one of the last questions (question 21), we asked respondents to choose, from a list of nine, which degrees are offered at their institutions, while allowing respondents the ability to check all that apply. The top three most common degrees chosen were Master of Arts (MA) (20.7%, n = 54), Bachelor of Arts (BA) (18%, n = 47), and Master of Divinity (MDiv) (17.2%, n = 45).

Findings

In addition to inquiring about professional and institutional contexts, several survey questions asked respondents to indicate their primary means of gathering ideas for purchasing resources. Questions about methods of collection development included multiple response questions (questions 8 and 10), ranked choice questions (questions 9 and 11), and an open field question (question 7). Asking multiple response questions and ranked choice questions was an intentional aspect of the survey design as a way to reaffirm collection development methods that respondents had provided earlier in the survey through the open field question, while providing opportunities for them to expand beyond these primary techniques and offer other strategies that they employ. This section illuminates these responses and seeks to identify current collection development practices across the field.

Collection Development Funding

A total of 61 respondents answered that yes, the collections budget they receive satisfies the needs of religious studies or theology faculty and students at their institution (question 6; see figure 3). However, among the 45 comments respondents provided, 16 of these individuals indicated that they would buy more materials if they could. One respondent succinctly captured a theme among many respondents by saying, "We keep up with the necessities, but not luxuries." Five respondents indicated that donors or endowed gift funds allowed collection development needs to be met. Aside from collections budgets, two respondents specifically identified interlibrary loan (ILL) as meeting their information access needs, and two other responses stated that they rely on consortial purchases and couriers. Interestingly, three respondents stated that they have no budget specifically dedicated to religious studies or theology, and five respondents shared that they have a healthy budget that, for one respondent, "more than satisfies the needs."

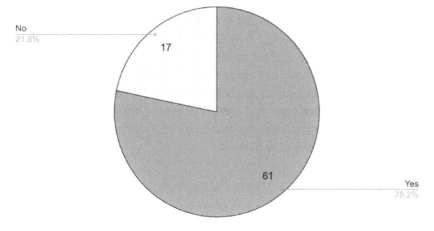

Does the collections budget you receive satisfy the needs of religious studies or theology faculty and students at your institution?

No
21.8%

17

61

Yes
78.2%

Figure 3: Represents the results of question 6.

Of the 17 respondents who said that their collections budget is not satisfying faculty and student needs, nine of them specifically stated they need more funds, and four explicitly stated that they are not meeting patron needs. Two respondents indicated that their funding has decreased in the recent past. One said, "As far as I know [we are meeting patron needs], however in the last ten years our collections budget in general has decreased significantly. I am sure they have noticed, but like much of campus, we are making do." Another respondent quantified the decrease in their collection development funds saying they have experienced "more than 50% budget reduction in the past 7 years." Three respondents also mentioned ILL as a means of meeting patron needs.

Methods of Collection Development

Prior to providing a list of answers from which respondents could choose, the researchers wanted to gather responses from an open-ended question (question 7): When considering possible acquisitions to the religious studies/theology collection, what is the primary method by which you discover relevant materials to add to the collection? With a total of 79 responses, this was a valuable question to ask as a way for respondents to focus on the purpose of the survey and especially because consecutive questions did not contain an exhaustive list of possible collection development methods.

Coding these responses revealed that faculty input and requests were the most frequently mentioned method by which respondents discovered relevant materials to add to the collection (n = 28) (see figure 4). Respondents also gathered suggestions from students (n = 8) and four respondents generated purchase ideas from patron requests in general. These patron requests could include faculty or students, but respondents did not specify these patrons in their responses. One respondent explained how they gather recommendations from faculty and students stating that they gather this information at "[q]uarterly and or annual meetings with faculty and students." The prevalence of faculty input and requests demonstrate that, among patron-motivated requests, faculty, rather than students, are setting the tone for collecting materials.

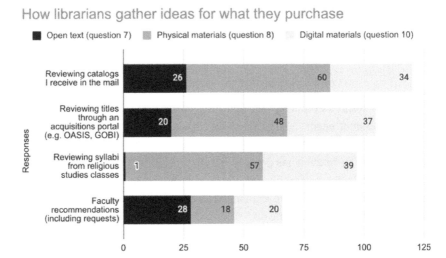

Figure 4: Represents themes coded from responses to question 7, juxtaposed with responses to questions 8 and 10.

Respondents were typically methodical in the way they approached collection development, indicating that they used acquisition tools (such as OASIS and GOBI) (n = 20), approval plans (some of which could have been through a platform such as OASIS or GOBI, however these were not explicitly named) (n = 9), reviewing publisher's catalogs (n = 26), and checking social media (n = 4). However, one respondent replied that their primary method of discovering materials was "serendipity."

Collecting Physical Materials

The most common way respondents identified gathering ideas about physical materials to purchase was by reviewing catalogs they received in the mail (n = 60) (see figure 4). The next most popular responses were reviewing syllabi from religious studies or theology courses (n = 57) and reviewing titles that match a pre-established profile through an acquisitions portal (such as ProQuest OASIS or GOBI) (n = 48). In addition to respondents choosing among a list of answers provided by the researchers, they could also describe other methods by which they gather ideas for purchase suggestions of physical materials. Respondents had the opportunity to choose "Other" and type their own responses in an open text field. Forty-two respondents chose to type their own responses. Popular responses included gathering purchase ideas from faculty requests (n = 18) and student recommendations (n = 8). Some novel responses included: hearing about books on Catholic radio and denominational news sources, a "cataloguer letting me know that we're missing volumes from a series," faculty reading (with one bemused, yet frustrated, respondent asking "WHY don't they tell me what they're reading!!??"), sermons and guest speakers on campus, and usage and turn-away statistics. When asked to rank the ways that they gather ideas about what physical items to purchase (question 9), respondents overwhelmingly chose "Reviewing titles that match a pre-established profile through an acquisitions portal (e.g., Proquest OASIS, GOBI)."

Collecting Digital Materials

The researchers were interested to learn if collection development practices differed based on the physical or digital format of the materials, particularly how librarians gathered ideas for purchasing each. There was a difference between the two, though librarians ranked methods similarly. The most popular method by which librarians reported gathering ideas to purchase digital materials was reviewing syllabi from religious studies classes (n = 39) (see figure 4)–the second most popular method for considering physical materials. The next most popular method for considering the purchase of digital materials was also a popular consideration for the purchase of physical materials–reviewing titles that match a pre-established profile through an acquisitions portal (such as ProQuest OASIS or GOBI) (n = 37). The most popular method for librarians to gather ideas for physical materials–reviewing catalogs they receive in the mail–was the third most popular method for librarians to consider purchasing digital materials (n = 34).

Forty-one respondents chose "other" and described additional considerations and their specific contexts. Like in the responses for sourcing ideas for physical materials, respondents also commonly referenced sourcing digital material recommendations from their patrons. These included faculty requests (n = 20), student requests (n = 4), and patron recommendations (where the respondent did not specify either faculty or student) (n = 3). Similar to results for the question about physical materials, two respondents said that they look to other libraries' holdings for ideas of digital materials to purchase. However, where consortial purchasing was not mentioned for physical materials, two respondents identified the importance of consortial purchasing for digital formats. One respondent specifically mentioned the importance of their e-book packages through the Association of Christian Libraries. Also, notably different from gathering ideas to purchase physical materials, respondents gathered ideas based on listservs, including the "Atla discussion list" (n = 3) and through patron-driven or demand-driven acquisition models (n = 3). Between mentions of consortial agreements, colleagues' suggestions, and generating purchase ideas from listservs, responses indicate that librarians may be more dependent upon, or simply more open to, collaborative collecting of digital materials.

Respondents also used this open text field to describe challenges to subscribing to digital content and funding annual fees. One respondent indicated they pay less attention to digital materials overall, stating, "I don't tend to order e-books, and databases are too expensive to justify," while another wrote that ordering digital materials is based on funding:

> When I can get funding for a larger purchase, some of the Brill encyclopedias, such as *Textual History of the Bible Online, Encyclopedia of Jewish History and Culture* are core. I cannot pay for anything that has a substantial annual maintenance or subscription fee.

Whether due to cost, patron preferences, or user needs, one respondent stated that they "rarely buy individual e-books and rarely subscribe to a new database."

Challenges of Acquisitions Tools

Coming from a university setting that uses Proquest OASIS as a means of both discovering print and e-book titles to purchase and actually making that purchase, we were interested in learning what obstacles other librarians face in using an acquisitions tool such as Proquest OASIS or GOBI. For those who, for either question 8 or 10, did not choose the option "Reviewing titles that match a pre-established profile through an acquisitions portal (e.g., Proquest OASIS, GOBI)" as a means of gathering ideas for titles to purchase, we asked respondents to comment on what prevents them from using such tools (question 12). Forty responses were recorded and, of those, 17 actually said that they do use an acquisition tool. GOBI was more popular, with 15 respondents using it. OASIS was much less popular, with only three respondents disclosing that they use it, and all three of those users also using GOBI. There was an overall familiarity with GOBI, where even those who did not use an acquisitions tool mentioned it by name, but there was a lack of use and familiarity with OASIS, including two of the 40 respondents, who had not heard of that product. Of the 17 respondents who do use an acquisitions tool such as GOBI or OASIS, five mentioned that they only use it for processing or ordering specific materials and not to generate ideas for purchases. Users also often disclosed an exception to their use of such a tool. For example, one respondent said that they cannot order books from Israel because they are not available through GOBI, and another stated, "I do use it in some limited ways but not for e-resources."

Barriers to use included lack of time to gain familiarity with these tools ($n = 4$), and eight respondents commented that they did not see a need to use these tools. Reflecting this, one respondent stated, "I don't feel they are needed at this time. I am comfortable with how I have been doing it." Some respondents said that using these tools is "not worth it." Six responses were coded as such and, alluding to a dimension of complexity, included comments such as "[it's] too much hassle to set it up" and "it seems to add another layer to the process that doesn't need to be there." Another barrier to using these tools is cost. Five respondents expressed that these tools are too expensive, one going so far to say that "they overcharge for their services." One notable response mentioned cost and issues that contributed to a change in their workflow. They said, "We used GOBI in the past. However, since we order books via Amazon, we could not justify the cost of GOBI. We also had some issues with the GOBI alerts." A few other respondents mentioned challenges to using these products effectively, stating that "they are not user friendly," and one librarian stated that the tool they used "never worked well for my predecessors and I was unable to get it to work well." Though these responses expressed strong opinions, only four respondents expressed difficulty in using an acquisitions tool.

Additional Considerations...

...about Collection Development Practices

After collecting answers to respondents' primary means of gathering ideas to inform purchases, the researchers wanted to provide an opportunity for librarians to share any additional comments about their collection development practices (question 14). The 32 responses varied greatly, but a few themes and individual responses are worth noting here.

Several respondents (n = 4) commented on the evolution of collection development. One indicated that their approach to collecting has shifted from a "just in case" model to "more of a 'just in time' model" where they "heavily depend on ILL, syllabi, and faculty for purchase suggestions." Another respondent acknowledged that expense is an issue and described changes in collecting as a result of needing to "decrease costs as much as possible," and how this is very "different from ten or 20 years ago." An environment where expense is a prominent concern may also motivate responses such as this one, from a librarian who uses statistics to rationalize purchases: "Based on analysis of circulations and usage, we know that we should buy much more in Bible and homiletical prep than in, say, historical theology or church history. Usage matters greatly in how I select new materials." One librarian noted that, in the current purchasing landscape, acquisition may be driven directly by patrons themselves with "Print and Electronic Demand Driven" models where "patrons can order without Librarian mediation." Another respondent, after answering the question about using acquisition tools (question 12), took the opportunity to emphasize that "there is a whole world out there that GOBI does not supply. Harrasowitz and Aux Amateurs have interesting material. I used to select from them and from Casalini before funding plummeted. Israeli publications are also pertinent and excellent. They are not covered in GOBI."

While eight respondents stated they rely heavily on faculty requests, several expanded and provided insight on the nature of engaging them. These librarians provided glimpses into their relationships with faculty. One respondent mentioned sending personalized emails several times within a year "asking for their input on specific titles and encouraging them to suggest other ones," and another mentioned that they previously used an approval plan through GOBI, but opted out of it and "now mainly handle faculty requests." Additionally, discussions with faculty yielded a greater understanding of faculty needs, however, these needs can look very different depending on the institution. From one respondent's experience, "[w]hen I ask faculty whether I should buy the print book or the ebook, they invariably prefer print," yet another librarian at a different institution stated that "most monographs we buy are e-books." Another respondent indicated an overall trend gathered from their faculty, stating that "[t]here is less of a push for individual titles and more wishes for databases and electronic journals." Although answers throughout the survey have indicated that faculty requests are an important way to gather ideas for purchases, it is important to acknowledge that librarian-disciplinary faculty relationships differ between institutions. For some, building relationships with faculty is an ongoing process and it can be challenging to gain faculty buy-in. One respondent stated that, although they receive "a lot of feedback from faculty," their "biggest struggle... is getting faculty to send me book requests."

Leveraging relationships may also be present internally as librarians navigate administrative priorities and purchasing workflows. Two librarians specifically noted that administrative barriers impact their collection development practices, where one librarian's "administration has made it clear that instruction and reference are more important, so I don't devote a ton of time to it," and another respondent stated that their "practices are hampered by some profound misunderstandings on the part of institutional administrators." Other librarians, such as this respondent who disclosed they are a part of an affiliate library, must engage additional colleagues as "large journal subscriptions are handled through the main university's library (as they have more buying power)."

Two additional notable responses are grounded in librarianship values of access and inquiry. One librarian expressed a desire to problem-solve issues of access, stating that they "[w]ould love to figure out how to turn some required course reserve material into ebooks when they are not available in that format from the publisher or out of print but still in copyright." Mirroring the ACRL's (2016) *Framework for Information Literacy*, which suggests that librarians and students alike view inquiry as engaging in scholarly conversations, another respondent stated that their collection development practice is grounded in "a deep understanding of the theological conversation over time."

...about Professional or Institutional Contexts

As with question 14, the researchers wanted to give respondents ample opportunity to describe their own unique circumstances by asking if they had any additional comments to add about their professional or institutional contexts (question 22). Many (n = 28) provided a more nuanced glimpse into their own settings, sharing more information on the population they serve, historical facts about their settings, and the structure of religious studies/theology at their institutions. Three respondents specifically commented on the interdisciplinary nature of the field: one mentioned a relationship with their philosophy department on campus; another stated that "Religious studies is actually a program at my university, not a department, so all our faculty are affiliated with some other department (soc, history, classics, etc);" and a third respondent detailed how the faith-based curriculum "places a high priority on faith integration across the disciplines," driving the collection development not only of theological materials, but also of "select theological resources related to a broad-range of academic disciplines." The second respondent mentioned the complexity of interdisciplinarity when it intersects with collection development, stating that "book ordering [is] complicated because faculty don't always think to contact me when their main liaison is in one of those other disciplines."

Interestingly, two respondents specifically named the presence of young disciplinary faculty as a source of hope for the growth of the field on their campus, with each of them stating that, although they currently do not offer a graduate program, they expect they will before long. In contrast, two other respondents focused on the broader landscape of information and higher education, offering more pessimistic views, with both comments relating to funding. One respondent stated, that "[w]e live in an information rich society that cannot afford to fund theological education," while another offered that "religion tends to be in the humanities part of universities. The humanities are not doing well these days, not in enrollments and not in university funding."

Three respondents indicated that they did not know the number of students pursuing undergraduate religious studies degrees at their institutions. This raises questions about the prevalence of this institutional data (one respondent stated that this number was not published) and methods librarians use to become familiar with and address the needs of their students.

Limitations and Further Areas of Inquiry

While this study broadly captured the current collection development practices of religious studies and theology librarians, it is important to note a few limitations of the study that may prevent the full realization of this goal.

First, the scope of this study could be expanded. We focused on recruiting librarians through the Atlantis listserv and by reviewing a list of ARL institutions. Recruiting through professional organizations, such as the Association of Christian Librarians (whose librarian members may or may not subscribe to the Atlantis listserv), or engaging in a more thorough review of institutions of higher education, especially with less of a research focus, in the United States and Canada could have been helpful. Additionally, we could have systematically gone through the listing of 278 ATS-accredited schools to research the librarians employed there and contacted them directly (similar to our recruitment of ARL librarians). Broader participation may have garnered more insight into collection development trends.

Additionally, aside from the first two questions, we did not require respondents to answer questions. Not answering every question resulted in a more limited understanding of professional and institutional contexts. For example, we did not require respondents to indicate their institution's religious affiliation, nor did we force respondents to share if they were from an ARL library or otherwise. Ultimately, this decision meant that not every respondent answered every question, especially the open text questions which invited participants to share more individualized experiences. We were grateful that, in one of these open text questions, many respondents chose to add the fact that they gather collection development ideas from patrons, especially through faculty and student requests. While this is an obvious and commonly used collection development method and we should have included it in our list of options, the impossibility of making available an exhaustive list of responses in questions 8 and 10 was complemented by the respondents who did choose to answer open text questions.

Although we attempted to present a comprehensive list of religious studies- or theology-related degrees as responses to question 21, respondents provided even more degree options in the open text question 22. One respondent stated, "We also offer these degrees: MA Christian leadership; MA Religion; MDiv/MA Counseling; MDiv/MA Conflict transformation; MDiv/MA Restorative justice," while another simply listed additional degrees offered: "Doctor of Missiology; Masters in Pastoral Ministry; Religious Education."

Future studies could investigate additional themes relevant to the ever-evolving field of librarianship. For example, we did not ask participants to identify how the open access movement is impacting their collection development practices. This is a major area of further research that should be studied. Additionally, especially as Atla membership expands around the world, it would be interesting to collect data from libraries located beyond the United States and Canada. Collecting this data would illuminate international collection development concerns and priorities, and it would allow for comparison of collection development trends on an international basis. Relatedly, it would be interesting to further explore the implications of distance education on collection development trends, especially considering this response to question 22: "We teach DMin and Master of Arts in Youth Ministry in 'intensive' mode. Most of the time, these students are on campus (or in the same state). This fact informs format decisions (get an e-book versus buy print)." Considering that some librarians stated that their patrons prefer print and others indicated that their patrons prefer electronic resources over print, information consumption and use trends should continue to be monitored and periodically studied.

Conclusion

The vast experience of the librarians who responded to the survey resulted in a current snapshot of the many ways religious studies and theology librarians engage in collection development practices. Further research on how these collection development practices align with the current needs of religious studies and theology scholars and students can be explored and used to inform professional development for librarians of all career stages. Awareness of a variety of trends is especially important to early career librarians who may be inexperienced in collection development and also able to think of new ways to identify and meet patron needs.

* * *

The authors would like to acknowledge the support of Dr. Ian Burke, Adam H. Lisbon, Tawny Burgess, and Gama Viesca.

Works Cited

Alt, Martha S. 1991. "Issues in Developing a Religious Studies Collection." *Library Acquisitions: Practice & Theory* 15, no. 2: 207–14.

American Library Association. 1999. *Libraries: An American Value.* www.ala.org/advocacy/intfreedom/americanvalue.

Association of College & Research Libraries. 2016. *Framework for Information Literacy for Higher Education.* Association of College & Research Libraries. www.ala.org/acrl/standards/ilframework.

Association of Theological Schools Commission on Accrediting. 2015. *Standards of Accreditation.* www.ats.edu/uploads/accrediting/documents/standards-of-accreditation.pdf.

Cooper, Danielle, Roger Schonfeld, Richard Adams, Matthew Baker, Nisa Bakkalbasi, John G. Bales, Rebekah Bedard, Chris Benda, Beth Bidlack, Sarah Bogue, Trisha Burr, Gillian Harrison Cain, Ina Cohen, Wesley Custer, Virginia Dearborn, Gerrit van Dyk, Suzanne Estelle-Holmer, Kathryn Flynn, Jennifer Gundry, Trevan Hatch, Justin Hill, Bill Hook, Thad Horner, Hye-jin Juhn, Andrew Keck, Michael Kohut, Gloria Korsman, Graziano Krätli, Ryan Lee, Rebecca Lloyd, Reed Lowrie, Margot Lyon, Jean McManus, John Meeks, Christine Pesch Richardson, John Robinson, Kay Roethemeyer, Robert Roethemeyer, Ramona Romero, Fred Rowland, Veronica Simms, Kate Skrebutenas, Jacqueline Solis, Steven Squires, Maria Stanton, Naomi

Steinberger, Chris Strauber, Elka Tenner, Amanda Thomas, Paul Allen Tippey, Nancy Turner, and Nicholas Weiss. 2017. "Supporting the Changing Research Practices of Religious Studies Scholars." Ithaka S+R. *doi.org/10.18665/sr.294119*.

Gregory, Vicki L. 2019. *Collection Development and Management for 21st Century Library Collections: An Introduction*. Second edition. Chicago: ALA Neal-Schuman.

Hook, William J. 1991. "Approval Plans for Religious and Theological Libraries." *Library Acquisitions: Practice & Theory* 15, no. 2: 215–27. *doi.org/10.1016/0364-6408(91)90057-L*.

Knievel, Jennifer E. and Charlene Kellsey. 2005. "Citation Analysis for Collection Development: A Comparative Study of Eight Humanities Fields." *The Library Quarterly* 75, no. 2: 142–68. *doi.org/10.1086/431331*.

Little, Geoffrey. 2012. "Collection Development for Theological Education." In *Library Collection Development for Professional Programs: Trends and Best Practices*. Edited by Sara Holder. IGI Global. *doi.org/10.4018/978-1-4666-1897-8.ch007*.

Schmersal, David E., Gerrit van Dyk, and Kaeley McMahan. 2018. "Back to Basics: Collaborating with Colleagues to Connect Graduate Students with Content." *ATLA Summary of Proceedings* 72: 141–50.

Shirkey, Cindy. 2011. "Taking the Guesswork out of Collection Development: Using Syllabi for a User-Centered Collection Development Method." *Collection Management* 36, no. 3: 154–64. *doi.org/10.1080/01462679.2011.580046*.

Appendix 5A: Survey Instrument

Collection Development Trends of Religious Studies and Theology Librarians

Thank you for participating in this research study! The researchers are interested in learning about religious studies and theological collection development trends in libraries in institutions of higher education throughout the United States and Canada.

1) Are you responsible for purchasing materials to support the study of religion or theology at your institution? (Y - next question/N; If No - end survey)

2) Is your institution located in the United States or Canada? (Y/N; If No - end survey)

Collection Development Practices

This first set of questions asks you to consider your institutional context and your own collection development practices as they relate to the purchase of religious studies or theology materials.

3) How do you fund the purchase of materials that support religious studies or theological scholarship? (check all that apply)
- ☐ a) Library's collections budget
- ☐ b) Disciplinary faculty fund purchases
- ☐ c) Institutional grants
- ☐ d) External grants
- ☐ e) Donors

☐ f) Other: _____

4) At your institution, what is the collections budget that supports religious studies or theological scholarship?
☐ Less than $1,000
☐ $1,001 – $5,000
☐ $5,001 – $10,000
☐ $10,001 – $15,000
☐ $15,001 – $20,000
☐ More than $20,000

5) Are funds for one-time purchases distinct from funds that support subscription-based resources (e.g., journals)?
☐ Yes
☐ No

6) Does the collections budget you receive satisfy the needs of religious studies or theology faculty and students at your institution?
☐ Yes, please comment: _____
☐ No, please comment: _____

7) When considering possible acquisitions to the religious studies/theology collection, what is the primary method by which you discover relevant materials to add to the collection?

Thinking about the acquisition of *physical materials* (e.g., books, DVDs), please respond to the following:

8) I gather ideas for what I should purchase from (check all that apply):
☐ a) Reviewing syllabi from religious studies classes
☐ b) Reviewing titles that match a pre-established profile through an acquisitions portal (e.g., Proquest OASIS, GOBI)
☐ c) Reviewing catalogs I receive in the mail
☐ d) Reviewing catalogs that disciplinary faculty give to me
☐ e) Reviewing lists of titles curated by vendors
☐ f) Attending discipline-specific conferences (e.g., AAR/SBL)
☐ g) Attending library conferences (e.g., Charleston conference, Atla Annual)
☐ h) Direct communications (emails or phone calls) from vendors
☐ i) Direct communications (emails or phone calls) from authors
☐ j) Reviewing books for a publication or professional organization (e.g., for Choice Reviews)

☐ k) Other (please describe): _____

9) Follow up from previous question: Please rank each of the ways you gather ideas (most frequent to least frequent)

Thinking about the acquisition of *digital materials* (e.g., eBooks, databases), please respond to the following:

10) I gather ideas for what I should purchase from (check all that apply):
☐ a) Reviewing syllabi from religious studies classes
☐ b) Reviewing titles that match a pre-established profile through an acquisitions portal (e.g., Proquest OASIS, GOBI)
☐ c) Reviewing catalogs I receive in the mail
☐ d) Reviewing catalogs that disciplinary faculty give to me
☐ e) Reviewing lists of titles curated by vendors
☐ f) Attending discipline-specific conferences (e.g., AAR/SBL)
☐ g) Attending library conferences (e.g., Charleston conference, Atla Annual)
☐ h) Direct communications (emails or phone calls) from vendors
☐ i) Direct communications (emails or phone calls) from authors
☐ j) Other (please describe):

11) Follow up from previous question: Please rank each of the ways you gather ideas (most frequent to least frequent).

12) If b is unselected in 8 and 10: What prevents you from using acquisitions tools such as OASIS or GOBI?

13) How do you gather purchase suggestions from library patrons? (check all that apply)
☐ a) Through personal communication (e.g., email request, hallway conversations)
☐ b) I maintain a purchase request submission form
☐ c) My institution maintains a purchase request submission form
☐ d) When faculty request items to be purchased for course reserves
☐ e) I circulate vendor catalogs among disciplinary faculty
☐ f) Other (please describe): _____

14) Do you have any additional comments about your collection development practices that you would like to add?

Professional & Institutional Context

This final set of questions asks you to describe your professional and institutional context.

15) At what stage are you in your career?
- ☐ Early career
- ☐ Mid-career
- ☐ Advanced career
- ☐ Nearing retirement

16) Please choose the answer which best describes your institution below:
- ☐ Public university or college
- ☐ Private university or college
- ☐ Private religiously affiliated university or college
- ☐ University- or college-affiliated divinity school
- ☐ Stand-alone seminary
- ☐ Other: _____

17) What is the total enrollment (undergraduate and graduate) at your institution?
- ☐ Less than 1,000
- ☐ 1,001 - 5,000
- ☐ 5,001 - 10,000
- ☐ 10,001 - 15,000
- ☐ 15,001 - 20,000
- ☐ 20,001 - 25,000
- ☐ 25,001 - 30,000
- ☐ 30,001 - 35,000
- ☐ More than 35,000

18) Which, if any, religious tradition and denomination is your institution affiliated with:
- ☐ Open text box: _____
- ☐ Not applicable

19) What is the approximate number of undergraduate students seeking degrees in religious studies or theology at your institution?
- ☐ Less than 25
- ☐ 26–50
- ☐ 51–100

☐ More than 100

☐ Not applicable

20) What is the approximate number of graduate students seeking degrees in religious studies or theology at your institution?

☐ Less than 25

☐ 26–50

☐ 51–100

☐ More than 100

☐ Not applicable

21) What are the religious studies or theology degrees granted by your institution (check all that apply):

☐ a) PhD - Doctor of Philosophy

☐ b) ThD - Doctor of Theology

☐ c) DMin - Doctor of Ministry

☐ d) MDiv - Master of Divinity

☐ e) MATS/MTS - Master of Arts in Theological Studies/Master of Theological Studies

☐ f) MA - Master of Arts

☐ g) MARS - Master of Arts in Religious Studies

☐ h) ThM - Master of Theology

☐ i) BA - Bachelor of Arts

22) Do you have any additional comments about your professional or institutional context that you would like to add?

Thank you for completing this survey!

[Submit]

If you would like to receive a summary of the survey results, please enter your email address below. Note that all email addresses will be kept separately from survey responses and they will not be used to identify your answers to our questions.

Email address:

——

CHAPTER 6

Giving Libraries Their Due

A Call for a Morally Serious Process for Libraries in Transition

STEPHEN D. CROCCO, YALE DIVINITY LIBRARY

*I*n recent decades, pressures and opportunities led many theological schools to dramatically reshape themselves and, by extension, their libraries. Budget constraints, novel degree programs, fresh approaches to teaching and learning, new kinds of students, changing space needs, and schools closing or merging have kept a growing number of libraries in states of transition. In most cases, these transitions led to a reduction in the size and the scope of library spaces and collections; only rarely have pressures and opportunities led schools to add space for libraries. In 2017, the Association of Theological Schools (ATS) reported, "Since 2010, 27 schools (10% of the ATS membership) have merged, embedded, or otherwise affiliated. Embedded schools now represent about 39% of the membership. At the current pace, in a few years, the majority of ATS schools will be embedded" (2018, 10). Affiliations, for schools embedding portions of their institutions and for schools receiving those portions, are complex undertakings, even when things go smoothly. They involve extensive negotiations about faculty positions, severance payments, endowments, and governance. By embedding, schools that cannot survive or thrive on their own get new leases on life even if they struggle with a sense of loss and questions about their identity moving forward. For schools with adequate resources but without clear ways forward, embedding provides opportunities to reposition themselves and play to their strengths. Receiving schools get an infusion of resources which could include students, faculty members, property, donor records, endowment funds, library materials, and the reputations of their new partners.

The argument of this chapter is that libraries facing major transition–such as being dismantled, radically reduced in size, or embedded in another institution– deserve more than a brief ceremony to acknowledge with gratitude the end of one library story and possibly the beginning of another. If the sentiments behind such ceremonies are real–and who in theological education does not profess love for libraries–libraries deserve something more. They need to be shown respect in the form of a morally serious process that guides the transition from beginning to end. Like any process, the one described here depends upon identification of specific issues in the transition, open communication about shared outcomes, preparation and planning, attentive follow-through, and evaluation. It also requires serious attention to the status of collections themselves.

In its simplest form, a *process* is anything that stands as a bulwark against wishful thinking and hasty decisions on the part of stakeholders–librarians included –who resist the hard facts of what is about to take place or who fail to see the potential of what should or could take place. A *serious* process is necessary because a sentimental fondness for libraries and a vision for what could or should take place in a transition can easily give way when hard deadlines and bottom lines come into play. A *morally* serious process stresses that there are issues beyond logistics–communication, planning, and follow-through–that have to do with the literature of theology itself and an obligation to preserve certain expressions of it. A basic question in a transition is not just what is possible but also what is desirable. Opportunities to combine historic and historical collections are rare and important enough to put claims of "Impossible!" on hold, at least temporarily. This may be the one occasion when two schools need to do the impossible, even if that means bringing other institutions and organizations into the picture. The process described here for libraries in transition lays out an argument to secure the best possible outcomes for the libraries, the schools, for theological education generally, and even for the literature of theology.

Libraries in Transition

The decision to dismantle, reduce, or embed a theological library raises a host of intellectual and moral concerns that stressed schools facing constraints and deadlines are tempted to reduce to logistics. Libraries in transition are particularly vulnerable to rushed planning and wishful thinking because they are rarely front and center in anyone's mind other than the minds of the librarians. Given their sheer materiality and sophistication, libraries are the least agile parts of theological schools. For that reason, depending on the desired outcome, efforts to responsibly downsize or embed libraries may be the most complex and time-consuming parts of an affiliation process, though they are rarely seen that way by non-librarians.

This chapter is informed by my involvement with the embedding of Andover Newton Theological School (ANTS) into Yale Divinity School (YDS) in 2017. While the experience did not involve every aspect of transition faced by libraries, it offered enough to have some value as "lessons learned" or as an "after-action report." Leading up to the embedding, it was no secret that ANTS had financial difficulties. It seemed unavoidable that ANTS's campus would be sold and the Trask Library would need to be in a position where it could be vacated in short order, whether the school had identified a new future or not. Several years before its agreement with YDS, the ANTS librarian was instructed by its president to prepare the library for a future that was not yet foreseen. I came to the Yale Divinity Library (YDL) in the fall of 2015, just when conversations between ANTS and YDS began in earnest. Around then, high-level teams from both schools–presidents, deans, trustees, financial officers, and attorneys–met weekly and gave a great deal of attention to every aspect of an embedded relationship except the libraries. According to the ANTS president, that task was being handled by the school's librarian. The dean of YDS displayed a similar confidence in his librarian to make any arrangements necessary or desirable with the ANTS library. An agreement between the two schools was touch-and-go until late in the process. The YDL struggled to match its level of preparation with the likelihood of an agreement, which fluctuated considerably over time. By the time the matter was all but certain, ANTS made many unilateral decisions about its library services and collections. When the two institutions completed the embedding process in spring 2017, ANTS's extensive special collections and several thousand circulating volumes moved to New Haven. The ANTS library now lives and, in real ways, thrives in the YDL, which is greatly enriched by its materials.

Done well, a thoughtful affiliation process dignifies the closing of the embedding library as a separate entity, infuses life into the receiving library, and may give life to new and existing libraries throughout the world. Done poorly, an affiliation process will put the embedding and receiving libraries through unnecessary hardships and squander opportunities. An analogy may help. A library collection about to undergo a radical transition is like an organ donor who is about to die. The striking picture below, of surgeons surrounding a patient, illustrates the need to meld logistical and moral concerns.

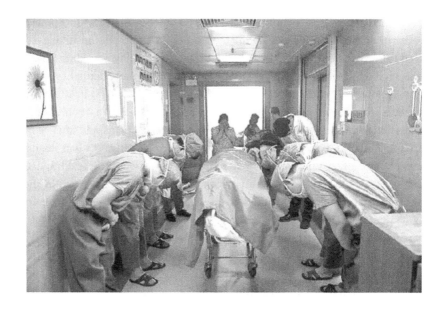

Here bowing is a show of respect for the child who has just died and for his grieving mother. For the sake of the analogy, I also infer that bowing is a show of mutual respect and humility between the surgeons who have agreed to work together in the grim, but life-giving, work ahead. It may be that the bowing figure not wearing scrubs is looking out for the best interests of the patient even in death by ensuring that the wishes of the patient-as-donor and the donor's family are respected, or perhaps that person functions as a transplant coordinator whose job it is to ensure cooperation between the surgeons to maximize beneficial results. One of the ways people make peace with the untimely deaths of loved ones is to know that their organs gave life or health to others. Imagine the tragedy and scandal that would occur if a hospital wasted donated organs because they could not orchestrate the necessary surgical procedures, or, much more horrifically, if the declaration of the death of a patient was tied to the needs of a transplant surgeon. There is more to transplant surgeries than technique and logistics; gratitude, honor, thoughtfulness, and respect come into play. Without acknowledging the moral dimensions associated with life, death, and life again, something important is lost.

When an institution beloved by many is about to die, it makes sense to use the language of right and wrong in their moral senses, not just as descriptions of technique. A library, especially one that has been assembled, funded, and cared for over a long history, is a unique cultural treasure, a wonder–a miracle even. Large numbers of people still see libraries with visible stacks of books and comfortable places to read them as magical and amazing places. Jorge Luis Borges (1989) continues to be quoted widely: "I was imagining Paradise as a kind of library." Disposing of a library collection carries far more moral weight than recycling metal bookshelves or discarding old library carrels. Imagine the reaction if a school's administration, pressed by time to empty its library building, waited until 5:00 a.m. on a Sunday morning to load its collection into a line of dump trucks headed for a paper recycler. When word got out, the news would be met with howls of disapproval by students and faculty members as well as the surrounding community. Unhelpful sentimental notions–that books are sacred and that discarding them is akin to burning them–come into play here and need to be overcome. Of all people, librarians know that printed materials have a lifespan, after which point it is permitted and often necessary to discard or recycle them. But treating a library collection as paper to be recycled for the sake of expediency would be widely condemned as a moral outrage.

Communication about Goals and Outcomes

Given the pressures on transitioning libraries, it is surprisingly easy to avoid questions, let alone extensive conversations, about goals and outcomes. ANTS and YDS librarians did not have the time or bandwidth to consider the best outcome potentially available to them. Faculty members and administrators showed little interest in the question, perhaps trusting that the librarians would know the answers. The one exception was ANTS's well-known collection of Jonathan Edwards manuscripts, which was mentioned frequently in discussions about the benefits of the possible affiliation. A process-related solution is simple enough. Librarians should have some regular representation on the committee overseeing the transition between the two schools and serve on an ad hoc library transition team that establishes goals, budgets, timelines, and procedures for evaluation. In the event of an impasse, a transition committee can serve as an arbiter. Depending on the complexity of the transition, it may be advisable to identify a project manager with a mandate and a budget to oversee the project.

Communication and collaboration between a range of stakeholders plays to the strengths of librarians and mitigates their weaknesses. Librarians are smart and hard-working, but they are only occasionally miracle-workers. As early as possible, a vision for what could and should be accomplished in the library affiliation needs to direct the way forward. Otherwise, expediency will dictate outcome and libraries will scramble. A faculty library committee–standing or ad hoc–would be a natural place to lodge the outcome question. Outcomes may have financial implications and an impact on facilities, so these decisions need to be coordinated with the larger committee.

It seems obvious that the librarians involved in an affiliation should lead the process, but it is worth noting that people skilled at working in libraries do not necessarily have the talent for dismantling or embedding them. If they have the talent they may not have the temperament to face overwhelming tasks, weighed down by the pressures of time and limited support. Even so, the day-to-day work and follow-through of embedding and receiving will lie with the schools' librarians. It also seems obvious that the two head librarians should run their own operations and make their own decisions, at least initially. But what does it mean for the process if the embedding library and its staff are destined to disappear from the picture? A process monitored by a library transition committee can ease potential bumps as the receiving library begins to assume control over the embedding library's materials–and it may be well before the moving vans show up. That scenario raises the potentially delicate issue of which institution is in charge and when. An embedding and receiving process puts huge demands on the two libraries, one of which is giving up something precious and the other is receiving, and perhaps being inundated by, something precious. It may be helpful to think about authority in terms of a sliding scale, where one librarian and library decreases while the other librarian and library increases. The affiliation process is not an instance of victim and victor, or of the rich taking from the poor. What it is, or what it should be, is an occasion where the embedding library is enabled to live again in a new, more stable, setting in the receiving library. Here the theme of resurrection is quite appropriate.

Preparation and Planning

Preparation and planning combine to form the foundation for showing respect to a library in transition. Every librarian knows that library work is detailed and complicated, but most others have little idea what goes on beyond the points of public service. In contrast, hospital transplant centers have skilled people, detailed procedures, and chain-of-command structures in place to anticipate, guide, and review decisions and actions. There are textbooks, codes of ethics, and best practices to guide activities and avoid pitfalls. Not surprisingly, there is little in the way of comparable literature and best practices for libraries in transition. For most theological libraries, dismantling and embedding collections are rare events. It would be unusual that anyone on either campus had first-hand experience, though that will undoubtedly change as the number of transitions increases. Twenty-first century administrators might reasonably assume there are computer programs that easily and accurately compare the holdings of two libraries, making collection development decisions and changes to respective databases easy. While there are electronic tools, they rarely produce accurate comparisons simply, quickly, and inexpensively. There are many high-touch procedures that take place in the transfer of volumes from one institution to another. In a library affiliation, there are dozens and dozens of issues, projects, and decisions which need attention.

A simple checklist or its equivalent will emerge as an essential tool for libraries in transition because there are too many things to remember and too many sequences to account for. Circulating a checklist will have the additional advantage of raising awareness among administrators who are ignorant of a library's intricacies and the complexities of an embedding process. As the project winds down, the checklist could turn into a punch list so that everyone is aware of the work still to be done once the formal papers of affiliation have been signed. Checklists are invaluable tools that should be passed from library to library, built up, and refined as time passes. If libraries continue to be dismantled and embedded as ATS predicts, perhaps Atla could draw on its members to help libraries conceive of new visions for themselves, establish best practices, and help find homes for good materials that are not needed or wanted by receiving libraries. An Atla ad hoc library transition advisory committee that meets on an on-call basis might be a good idea.

For individuals waiting on transplant lists, there is often no telling when appropriate organs will become available. People waiting for organs need to be prepared to receive them. There is a lesson here for libraries in the current climate. The possibility of a library's transition requires more than thinking about a process; it requires preparing for one. Giving libraries their due means librarians and senior administrators paying serious attention to libraries that may be transitioning before they reach that point. How likely is it that an institution will close or affiliate? How likely is it that an institution may be on the receiving end of part of a collection? All libraries at risk of being dismantled or embedded have good reasons to get as ready or agile as possible. Most libraries have backlogs of things that need to be done, along with aspirational backlogs of things that would be good to do. With any scent of affiliation in the air, librarians could decide whether to keep tapes and CDs of every chapel and holiday service since the 1950s, long runs of bound periodicals readily available on JSTOR, multiple copies of official school publications, and long-outdated reference works, to name a few examples. Presidents whose schools may need to transition should advise campus offices to clean out closets and file cabinets, sending specified kinds of materials to the school's archives. Before the need is urgent, schools could offer their libraries financial support for extra work-study students, temporary project archivists, and cataloging vendors to deal with materials that may have sat untouched for years.

A school that is a potential recipient of a library collection would also do well to prepare by addressing its own backlogs and materials of dubious value, freeing up space as it goes. It should also engage in thought experiments and planning exercises on how it might absorb a significant collection. Imagine a donor offering the most spectacular and useful collection a school could imagine, and all she wants to know is where you would put all 5,000 volumes. A receiving library could explore the feasibility of replacing regular shelves with a run of compact shelving, turning to donors who may be interested in special projects. Such planning might include identifying or creating some swing space for collections that may be received. YDL sent about 1,000 linear feet of bound periodicals to Yale's offsite library storage facility in anticipation of the possibility of ANTS materials coming to the YDL. Now that those materials have largely been absorbed, the space remains a permanent swing space for other collections and shifting projects.

In an affiliation, a newer school with a small library collection may use the opportunity to build up its numbers, while a school with a mature library may want or need very little. Many libraries in transition have large numbers of materials that are worth transplanting that are not needed or wanted by the receiving school. These materials warrant special consideration before being offered to a used book dealer or put on a book sale table. Schools with libraries facing a transition often struggle financially and may lack funds to support the work necessary to dismantle and embed their collections. Administrators may want to sell books to help pay some of the related costs. Trying to sell a library collection that cost hundreds of thousands, if not millions, of dollars over the years will likely lead to disappointment. Even with the proliferation of new theological schools in North America, there appears to be little or no market for entire library collections. A used book dealer who specializes in scholarly items may be interested in selecting a thousand choice volumes from a collection, leaving the remainder for a book sale table where proceeds will return dimes—if not nickels—on dollars. Proceeds from these sales may be enough to pay the scrap paper dealer to haul away what is left.

Instead of going the sales route early, a school should consider donating useful portions of its library to educational institutions in the Majority World and use the occasion to raise funds from alumni/ae proud to see their beloved library being used in such a thoughtful way. An even better development opportunity would be to send a somewhat intact library to a partner school overseas. There the library will live again, as deeply appreciated as it ever was, and may become one of the largest theological libraries in the country almost overnight. Keep in mind that dated materials, picked-over collections, and titles geared to a North American context are generally out of place overseas, the principle being that theological students and faculties overseas deserve the same quality and applicability of materials as their counterparts in North America. Not all regular circulating materials are suitable or desirable for embedding or donating. Just as surgeons reject diseased or worn-out organs for transplant, some library collections can be said to be suffering from disease or old age. After years of budget cuts, excessive weeding to save space, sales of rare and antiquarian books, heavy use of the collection, etc., there may be little worth transplanting to a healthy library or donating to a library overseas.

Attentiveness to Follow-through and Evaluation

In this chapter, I have laid the responsibilities for logistics at the feet of a library transition committee–a committee that has a voice at appropriate faculty and administrative levels and access to a budget for the process. With a logistical structure in place, some of the moral dimensions of libraries in transition can come to the fore. Two schools seeking to affiliate are likely to have similar or compatible theological traditions, but that does not mean that their collections will be identical. ANTS and YDS are both mainline Protestant schools that are historically related to the congregational roots of the United Church of Christ. It was a safe bet that there was considerable duplication between the two libraries. However, since the United Church of Christ was made up of two other denominations with different European roots–Evangelical and Reformed–an affiliation between a school out of one of those traditions and YDS would have been a different matter. In the case of ANTS, the YDL was enriched by strong holdings in the areas of Baptist history, evangelical theology, and ministry–none of which were collection strengths at Yale. ANTS's special collections would have come to the YDL if nothing else did. Antiquarian books and pamphlets, manuscript collections, and institutional archives were a priority because of the overlapping history between the two schools that began when Yale president Timothy Dwight helped found Andover Seminary in 1806. Treasures from the ANTS collection included strong holdings in mission history that added to the YDL's renowned holdings in that area and a collection of Jonathan Edwards manuscripts, which are now in the Beinecke Rare Book and Manuscript Library at Yale.

A morally serious and respectful process needs to focus on an embedding library's "special collections"–a blanket term for materials kept in restricted areas and used by patrons under the supervision of library staff. Special collections materials typically include institutional archives, unpublished collections of personal and organizational papers, photographs, rare and antiquarian books and pamphlets, and realia. Of these materials, pretty much everything but rare and antiquarian books and pamphlets are unique. Quite simply, that is why there is a moral obligation to preserve them somewhere. While the receiving library may be the ideal place, denominational historical societies or college or university libraries are also worth consideration.

The possibility of affiliation is also a good time to reassess a library's antiquarian and rare books. Many antiquarian books, even books hundreds of years old, are not rare and not monetarily valuable because they are not scarce. When so-called rare and antiquarian books can be readily found in other libraries or are available digitally from reliable sources, there may be good reasons to set aside a number for teaching purposes and displays and donate or sell the rest to libraries that can care for them. Things get complicated when considering the fate of rarely used books and pamphlets that are neither rare nor antiquarian. How do older and little-used materials impact a morally serious embedding process? The answer to this question varies with the goals of the receiving library and the amount of space it has available for collections. Does it see itself as a collection that primarily supports the curriculum and basic faculty research? Or does it aspire to support more advanced faculty research by holding primary source materials that often include obscure and dated books? Does it have or sense an obligation to preserve certain kinds of materials whether they are ever used? An example would be nineteenth-century materials from small immigrant denominations. A library may need to keep these items until they can be certain they are available in a library where they will be held in perpetuity or as microforms or in reliable electronic formats.

Final Thoughts about the Moral Status of Collections

For a brief time, it was a serious question whether the YDL would take anything from the ANTS library other than its special collections. Following that path would have made things much easier, though the YDL would have missed out on many good materials. In instances of affiliation where minimal materials are embedded or sent overseas, the question of what to do with, say, 50,000 volumes, is a daunting one. There will be a time for book dealers and friends-of-the-library book sales. Even the most determined and conscientious efforts to find homes for materials will end with a call to a paper recycler. But, after sending materials overseas and before getting the friends of the library to set up a monster book sale, the morally serious process described in this chapter points to one more thing. An underlying assumption of this chapter is that the literature of theology contains within itself a moral imperative to be preserved for posterity. Otherwise we lose the voices of those who preceded us in the faith. Libraries are places where those voices are kept and treasured. Being reasonably certain that unwanted materials are preserved somewhere is one way we honor our parents in the faith. It is how we honor the history of scholarship to which all theological schools are committed to some degree.

Admittedly, the task of identifying materials that might be at risk of being lost is almost impossible with the pressures associated with an affiliation process. Perhaps the most that can be done is to assign someone to identify pockets of obscure, dated, quirky, scarce, and/or local publications among the remaining materials and verify that they are held somewhere. If they are unique or truly scarce, their rarity provides the justification and obligation to preserve them. When all is said and done, this may be the ultimate test of a morally serious affiliation process that gives libraries their due.

It was no surprise that ANTS and YDS held a public service to sign papers of agreement to celebrate their new relationship. I do not recall that anything was said about the libraries on that occasion. I wondered what might count as a suitable ceremony of appreciation for the new, merged library collection. A recognition service in the library? A lecture by a faculty member familiar with ANTS's history? YDL decided to celebrate the occasion by doing an exhibit featuring the history of ANTS. Looking back, the most appropriate way to respect the ANTS library–and the YDS library for that matter–may have been to bow when entering the library as a sign of respect for the great written traditions of the Christian faith that theological librarians are privileged to collect and study.

Works Cited

Association of Theological Schools. 2018. *Annual Report.*
   www.ats.edu/uploads/resources/publications-presentations/colloquy-
   online/2018-annual-report.pdf.
Borges, Jorge Luis. "Poema de los dones." In *Obras Completas*, vol. 2, 187–8.
   Buenos Aires: Emecé.
Shenzhen Evening News. 2014. "11-Year-Old Cancer Patient Donates Organs."
   china.org.cn, June 10, 2014. www.china.org.cn/china/2014–
   06/10/content_32621766_2.htm.

CHAPTER 7

Atla Down Under

The Impact of International Collaboration Between Atla and ANZTLA on Theological Librarianship

KERRIE STEVENS, ALPHACRUCIS COLLEGE (MELBOURNE, AUSTRALIA), AND SIONG NG, CAREY BAPTIST COLLEGE (AUCKLAND, NEW ZEALAND)

*T*he Australian and New Zealand Theological Library Association (ANZTLA) and Atla are two like-minded organisations on opposite sides of the planet, focused on very similar goals. The origins and history of Atla and ANZTLA also follow a very similar path, despite being separated by four decades. The commonalities of the progression, development, and growth of both associations have demonstrated familiar ups and downs for both.

ANZTLA's Origins

ANZTLA and Atla's origins begin in similar circumstances, although separated by about 40 years. ANZTLA started out of a series of special library consultations between the ANZATS (Australian & New Zealand Association of Theological Schools), the ANZSTS (Australian and New Zealand Society for Theological Studies), and the AASR (Australian Association for the Study of Religions). The fifth such consultation culminated with the official beginnings of ANZTLA in 1985 (Robinson 2010).

With a mission of "seek[ing] to foster the study of theology and religion by enhancing the development of theological and religious libraries and librarians," ANZTLA's history has always been focused on supporting the libraries and librarians of its membership. Working together, members have achieved great outcomes on behalf of the Association that have benefitted not only the relatively small theological library community but the wider library community as well.

Elliott (2006, 242) outlines that the beginnings of the then American Theological Library Association (now known as Atla) were discussed by the AATS (American Association of Theological Schools) in 1946–7. Comparing ANZTLA's mission to Atla's mission of "foster[ing] the study of theology and religion by enhancing the development of theological and religious studies libraries and librarianship," it is clear that the two associations are well and truly on the same path. The greatest shared characteristic between Atla and ANZTLA persisting to this day is collegiality (Bollier 2006, 234).

Twenty-two librarians and eleven representatives of theological colleges and seminaries witnessed the birth of ANZTLA. The meeting took place at Luther Seminary in North Adelaide (Zweck 1985). ANZTLA became officially established on Tuesday, August 27, 1985 (Zweck 1995). The following librarians formed the provisional executive of the association:

– President: Trevor Zweck
– Secretary/Treasurer: Hans Arns
– Executive member: Robert Withycome

The establishment of ANZTLA was not all smooth sailing. As early as the 1970s, stakeholders were in discussion about setting up ANZTLA. The President's report in 1987 stated that the constitutional questions with ANZATS had not been finalized. The report also highlighted the inability to secure a financial base ("Report on ANZTLA Inaugural Conference" 1987).

Conferences serve as a "forum where new ideas, proposed projects, and long-established interests" (O'Brien 2006, 252) can be shared, tested, and receive feedback for both associations. At the 1985 consultation, prior to ANZTLA being formally established ("Report on ANZTLA Inaugural Conference" 1987), Lawrence McIntosh delivered the keynote address. His paper, entitled "Professionalism in Theological Librarianship," emphasised the importance of the Australian Bibliographic Network (ABN) (Zweck 1995, 13). On the second day of the conference, Gary Gorman presented a practical workshop on collection development policy and practice. Hans Arns, on the other hand, presented a report with an international focus on European theological libraries (Zweck 1985, 71).

The first official ANZTLA Conference, held in Canberra from Monday, August 25 to Wednesday, August 27, 1986, saw several theological librarians gather to discuss topics such as: library standards, collection development and resource sharing, user education, and subject headings. Averil Edwards, the Chief Librarian from the National Library of Australia, delivered the keynote speech (Edwards 1988, 23). Twenty-six librarians reportedly attended the conference. This included two librarians from overseas: Don Huber from Ohio and Makis Dunni-ib of Lae, Papua New Guinea (Zweck 1995).

Similarly, the first Atla Conference, held in Louisville, covered topics such as the needs of theological libraries, the library's contribution to theological instruction, and cataloguing and classification (Elliott 2006, 243). Practical, helpful and useful session topics are features of each association's conference programs. Even the format of both association conferences has followed a similar schedule throughout the years: worship, devotional time (Elliott 2006, 244), and conference excursions are common to both (White 2006, 266).

Since their foundings, the constitutions of each association welcome membership from all libraries and librarians involved or interested in theological education, regardless of the tradition, denomination, or religion (Elliott 2006, 245). To demonstrate this, the first object of the ANZTLA Constitution is:

> to provide a framework whereby librarians and other people and groups interested in theological and religious libraries and librarianship can interact, learn and work towards the development and improvement of theological and religious libraries and the role and function of such libraries in theological education. (ANZTLA 2007)

Spirit and Ideals

Cooperation between libraries and librarians has been a constant feature for both associations. Elliott (2006, 246) describes the Atla Serials Exchange as an early tangible project completed by Atla members. ANZTLA members continue to offer duplicate periodicals between libraries, often at no cost, to enable each other to complete holdings and share duplicates in the most beneficial way possible.

The member values of both associations are strikingly common and could almost be interchanged. Both associations thrive on friendliness and cooperation, members who willingly accept responsibility for tasks that will benefit all, and a spirit of volunteerism in order to keep the associations functioning. Today, ANZTLA remains a voluntary association of professionals, whilst Atla moved to paid staff during the course of its development. We are "drawn together by some common interests and goals" because, generally, "we serve institutions that have a general educational goal of training persons for professional service in ministry" (O'Brien 2006, 251).

Atla is a considerably larger organisation with over eight hundred institutional, individual, and affiliate members, whilst ANZTLA has just over one hundred members at the time of writing. The majority of Atla members are located within the United States and Canada, though interest from outside the continent has increased in recent years. This has not always been the case. Paul F. Stuehrenberg, in his keynote address at the ForATL conference, reported that formerly Atla did not allow institutions or individuals outside of the United States and Canada to join (Stuehrenberg 2009). On the other hand, the majority of ANZTLA members are from Australia and New Zealand. ANZTLA also welcomes a handful of members from Pacific nations libraries who are eligible to apply for free ANZTLA membership through the Jeanette Little Scholarship Scheme (JLSS).

Atla and ANZTLA Collaboration, 1990–2020

Relationship Beginnings

Atla reached out to ANZTLA in 1990 when Richard H. Mintel attended and presented to the ANZTLA Conference held in Brisbane, Queensland (Mintel 1990). In 1995, Al Hurd, Atla Executive Director at the time, attended the ANZTLA conference in Canberra. Hurd (1996) presented a paper entitled "Maximizing Theological Resources" at that annual gathering. He also took the opportunity to attend the Australasian Religion Index (ARI) editorial board meeting on September 21, 1995 as an observer. His position and knowledge were greatly accepted and appreciated at the meeting. According to the minutes of the meeting, Hurd stated that VLTS (software), which was developed by Atla itself, had been developed and could be supplied to ARI at a lower cost. Hurd also indicated that Atla might be able to provide its thesaurus, to which Australian headings could be added. The Atla thesaurus became the subject descriptor source for ARI because it was "truer to the spirit of an index...; was reliable in its revisions; contained very many specialised religious terms not found in *LCSH*...; was consistent with [Atla's] *Religion Index One*; and was easy to manage and consult" (Harvey 1989, 18).

In recent years, the co-operation between our associations has steadily grown. In 2014, Brenda Bailey-Hainer, Atla Executive Director, accepted ANZTLA's invitation to be the keynote speaker for the 2014 Melbourne Conference, "Past, Present, Future." Since then, Maria Stanton, Atla Director of Production, has been a regular ANZTLA Conference attendee and was the keynote speaker at the 2018 Brisbane Conference, "Connecting People, Ideas, Learning." The title of her keynote address was "It's a Wonderful Library!" (Stanton 2018).

Conferences

A number of ANZTLA members have made an effort to attend Atla conferences over the years. The location of Atla conferences–usually the United States and occasionally Canada–does not seem to hinder members who see the importance of networking among fellow librarians from the other side of the world. As early as the mid–eighties, ANZTLA members realised the importance of professional development. In 1986, Trevor Zweck, the first president of ANZTLA, attended the 40th Atla conference in Kansas City, Missouri, held at Rockhurst College (Zweck 1987).

Prior to the conference, Zweck took the opportunity to meet Al Hurd, the preservation officer of Atla at the time. According to Zweck's wife, Pam, he recorded a meeting in his diary with Hurd on May 29, 1986 in Chicago. The main content of the meeting is not documented, but it is clear that the discussion related to Religion Index One and Two.

In his conference report, Zweck (1987, 8) stated that the Atla focal points were collection development and evaluation of applications and preservation. There were many highlights for Zweck, such as the denominational group meetings and hearing about the development to Atla Religion Indexes. Zweck also presented at the conference on June 17, 1986. His talk, entitled "Australian and New Zealand Theological Libraries and Librarianship" (Zweck 1986), received positive feedback and interest from theological education institutions and theological libraries.

The main highlight for Zweck was Michael Gorman's address on June 19, 1986, titled "Bibliographic Control in the Smaller, Specialized Library." Zweck (1987, 15) recommended to ANZTLA colleagues that it was essential for theological librarians to read this article when it was published in the *Proceedings*. Given by a compiler of AACR2, the talk encouraged librarians to conform to acceptable standards for the sake of sharing, despite each library having its own differences for its users. At the end of his own article, Zweck encouraged members of ANZTLA to attend future Atla conferences, as he saw the benefits of it.

According to Pam Zweck, her husband's attendance at the conference was followed by a visit to thirteen libraries in the United States that lasted for thirty-nine days. No doubt Zweck's involvement in the wider context influenced his leadership during his decade-long term as president of ANZTLA. Following his premature death, the 1997 Atla conference included a reading of Zweck's memorial tributes during the members session (Olson 1997). This recognition is due to the close relationship and the partnership Zweck had with Atla.

In subsequent years, a number of ANZTLA members have attended Atla conferences, including Helen Greenwood, one of the founding members of ANZTLA, who attended the 1993 Atla conference in Vancouver. Theological library issues and solutions seem to be common conference topics, no matter where the theological library may be located.

Conference collegiality has increased over recent years. In 2016, Atla held its conference in Los Angeles, making it one of the easier locations for Australians and New Zealanders to get to. That year featured a record five attendees from ANZTLA member libraries. The 2019 Atla Annual in Vancouver also attracted four ANZTLA member attendees (Stevens, Ng, Derrenbacker, and Burn 2020). Various other Atla conferences over the years have welcomed ANZTLA members with open arms. The international grant for people living outside the US and Canada makes it possible for many ANZTLA members to attend. The strategic vision to offer an international grant, first established in 2006, resulted in international collaboration and partnership with professionals from other continents (G. H. Cain, pers. comm., October 30, 2019). Attendance at conferences helps to build relationships between both parties, resulting in collaboration on projects, publications, and conference presentations. International travel, particularly to and from Australia, can be very expensive due to the large distances that must be covered. Whilst Atla member attendance at the ANZTLA Annual Conference has been minimal, we realize and appreciate that Australia and New Zealand are a long way from just about everywhere else!

Sponsorships

ANZTLA initiated the Jeanette Little Scholarship Scheme (JLSS) in recognition of Jeanette Little "to honour her many years of dedicated work with theological librarians in the Pacific" (ANZTLA n.d.). The scholarship enables Pacific Island theological librarians, who would otherwise not be able to attend, to participate in the annual ANZTLA Conference and receive training and support. The fund receives contributions from a percentage of ANTZLA and conference profits each year. Over the years, the JLSS has enabled numerous theological librarians from the Pacific Islands to attend the ANZTLA Annual Conference.

In a 2017 ANZTLA board meeting, Maria Stanton (Atla) initiated the introduction in 2018 of the Atla-ANZTLA Scholarship to allow for additional librarians from the Pacific region to attend the ANZTLA conference. This developing cooperation between Atla and ANZTLA helps to grow and develop theological librarianship in an under-resourced area. Theological librarians from Fiji and Papua New Guinea are recipients of the scholarship and have reported on the immense value and benefits of attending the ANZTLA Conference. This would have been impossible for them without the scholarship assistance (Premadish 2018; Lola 2019).

Both the JLSS and Atla-ANZTLA Scholarships not only benefit the theological librarians successful in receiving them; they also provide an excellent opportunity for Australian and New Zealander theological librarians to gain a greater understanding into the issues and hindrances faced by theological librarians in our region. Hearing of issues such as limited electricity supply that impacts database searching and catalogue access, different cultural practices regarding the provision and distribution of information, and common issues such as budget limitations and lack of library staff respect, helps to build a common ground of collegiality and support between theological librarians throughout the Pacific region. Assistance can be requested by any member and others strive to assist as best they can, creating a community reliant on and supportive of each other in many ways.

Consortium Agreements

ANZTLA's consortium has been in place for many years, allowing for many smaller libraries to take advantage of buying power when many work together for journal and database subscriptions. Currently, consortium and bulk bargaining power are in place for EBSCO databases, Oxford Biblical Studies Online database, Alexander Press databases, and various SAGE journal subscriptions. Subscription costs to many titles and products individually would be beyond many member libraries. By working together, ANZTLA enables many libraries to have access to a number of products that greatly benefit staff and students.

This sense of co-operation has benefitted many ANZTLA member libraries since consortium implementation in 2003 (Millard 2010, 49), when a task group was set up to investigate access to the then ATLA Religion Database online and ATLASerials. Participation in the ANZTLA consortium has steadily increased from year to year ever since. ANZTLA library members subscribing to AtlaSerials benefit hugely as their users are able to access the wide range of resources from the database. This includes journal titles from the Pacific region such as the *ANZTLA EJournal, Australian Biblical Review, Australian eJournal of Theology,* and the *Australian Journal of Biblical Archaeology.*

Publications

Australasian Religion Index (ARI)

ANZTLA's Australasian Religion Index is the major product produced entirely by ANZTLA volunteers over the last thirty years. In 1993, Atla "expressed interest in producing a CD-ROM version of ARI" (Zweck 1993, 2) but later decided against it. ARI indexes theological serials primarily produced in Australia and New Zealand. Atla's Religion Database is a much broader and much larger index than the ANZTLA counterpart, but the aims behind each product are similar–to index articles, reviews, and essays in all fields of religion and theology. Similarly, "the ATLA Religion Index was started using volunteer librarians" (Bailey-Hainer 2014, 7) until the work was gradually taken over by staff employed by Atla.

ANZTLA EJournal

Formerly the *ANZTLA Newsletter* (1987-2007), the *ANZTLA EJournal* (2008–) is the main form of formal communication amongst the Australia and New Zealand association. It contains papers presented at the Annual Conferences, statistics collected annually from member libraries, and other submissions from members and others that are of great interest to the membership. Its main audience is ANZTLA members, but it would be of interest to theological librarians worldwide. It is similar to Atla's *Theological Librarianship* ejournal, but with a slightly more regional focus. Both are open access and free and, coincidently, both are hosted by Atla.

Hosting

Atla has enabled numerous ANZTLA publications and products to continue being produced through its hosting services. Since its online inception in 2008, the *ANZTLA EJournal* was hosted by the National Library of Australia (NLA) using the Open Journal Systems (OJS) platform. In 2014, the NLA stated that they were are unable to continue hosting the *ANZTLA EJournal*. ANZTLA faced an uncertain time trying to find a suitable replacement hosting solution. Atla came to the rescue and the *ANZTLA EJournal* moved to the Atla domain. The migration to a new domain in October 2015 was virtually seamless. The *ANZTLA EJournal* continues to be produced by ANZTLA member volunteers and is published twice per year. It is open access, continues to use OJS, and can be found at *serials.atla.com/anztla/*.

Other Publications

"So Great a Cloud of Witnesses" (McIntosh, Harvey & Pryor 1995) was produced by ANZTLA in 1995 to celebrate the immense contribution to theological librarianship of Dr. Lawrence D. McIntosh. It has also now been published open access by Atla,

which has made this publication available through Books@Atla Open Press–another example of the ongoing cooperation between our like-minded associations. The ebook has an updated synopsis by Philip Harvey and is accessible from the Books@Atla Open Press website. The digitization and hosting of this publication were only made possible by generous support from Atla.

It is a splendid show of cooperation that ANZTLA publications and products can be shared via this relationship with Atla. As a comparatively small organization, ANZTLA does not have the infrastructure nor negotiating power to deal with large vendors and utilizing this aspect of Atla's publication process has been mutually beneficial in many ways.

International Theological Librarianship Education Task Force

As far back as 1995, Al Hurd (1996) recognized that "no one theological library association or religion indexing agency by itself can survive." Although this related directly to the introduction of new technologies, the overall premise is as applicable today as it was then. The recent development of Atla's International Theological Librarianship Education Task Force (ITLETF), of which ANZTLA member Kerrie Burn is a member, aims "to strengthen and connect theological and religious studies librarians worldwide by identifying resources, creating educational opportunities, and developing skill-enhancement materials through collaborative efforts" (Atla 2018). A recent publication produced by the task force, *The Theological Librarian's Handbook* (Ćurić 2020) is designed for those new to the profession or who may have limited options for acquiring formal training. By allowing and encouraging ANZTLA members to contribute to such worthy areas of great importance to theological librarians, such as this task force, Atla is demonstrating the importance of, and commitment to, our ongoing cooperation.

In 2019, the task force piloted the first Atla International Theological Librarian Leadership Institute at the annual conference held in Vancouver, Canada. Three librarians from majority-world countries were selected as participants in the institute. The week-long experience included classroom teaching, conference participation and presentation, and touring several theological libraries in Vancouver. This initiative is one of the examples of Atla's (2015) vision to be globally recognized as a strategic collaborator with other theological library associations. ANZTLA is encouraging its members to be part of this international professional development partnership.

A Global Future for Theological Librarianship

Changes in Theological Education

No doubt many of us have noticed the numerous changes in theological education over the last century. Demands of the church and society, developments in information technology, and declining numbers of church attendance and stretched finances are some of the influences that have shaped these changes (Jones 2019, 41).

A number of institutions seem to have moved from offering traditional models of theological education to an interdisciplinary approach. Dietrich Werner supports this by stating that theological education should include a "living encounter with different cultural ways and idioms to read and interpret the Bible" (quoted in Kahl and Andrée 2017, 9). The shift mainly reflects the changes and challenges theological students are facing in a rapidly changing world. Learning theology within the context of a ministry and the ability to understand the culture in which they serve are crucial skills for successful ministry and longevity. Werner, who has been influenced by a number of theologians in his theological journey, further argues that theological education is a process of growing into a wider and more inclusive understanding of the realities of churches that is not restricted by denominational differences (Kahl and Andrée 2017, 7). This raises a challenge for us as theological librarians: how are we adapting to the changes in our day-to-day operations?

Traditionally, in both Australia and New Zealand, institutions tend to run their operations in isolation. However, in recent years, a rise in significant collaboration among institutions has resulted in the formation of consortia (Ball 2018, 97). The University of Divinity, Australian College of Theology (ACT), and other colleges incorporated into larger universities, such as Charles Sturt University, are examples of institutions working together (Ball 2018, 89). Such developments have involved libraries merging and new partnerships forming among different institutional libraries (Burn 2019).

Sharing Strengths

Theological libraries all over the world face similar issues and concerns. By working together, we can assist and help each other work through them. Theological libraries have been cooperating globally in negotiating with publishers and other groups for reduced prices and more equitable subscription rates for theological journals for decades (Harmanny 2016, 25).

Sharing knowledge is a strength of the Atla-ANZTLA relationship. ANZTLA members (and others from around the world) are encouraged to take on active roles within Atla, such as Board positions and membership in relevant task forces. Both associations utilize email discussion forums to pose questions, request assistance, share initiatives, and more. Willingness to accept feedback, comments, and assistance from each other is evident, with both Atla and ANZTLA members regularly contributing to the others' forums.

Continued Growth

Theological libraries in Europe have been working together for many years. As like-minded associations collaborate, the impact and reach of resources and staff strengths are beneficial to all (Hall 1997). There is room, too, for growth and further development of the collaborative relationship between ANZTLA and Atla. Sharing knowledge by contributing to each other's publications is an important and valuable way to share information and ideas. Participating in each other's events, such as conferences and professional development activities, can only stand to enhance our individual knowledge and expand our international reach as we create and develop international colleague networks through such opportunities.

Global collaboration between like-minded associations is important as it helps all participants to stay relevant and current. Our world is constantly changing and with that change come both opportunities and challenges. By working together, we can make the most of opportunities and confront challenges with a combined force, distributing the workload and enhancing the overall impact.

"Libraries have always worked in partnership to support their communities whoever and wherever they are with the diverse needs, that are often unique to that community, driving the offerings of that service" (Paull n.d.). The theological library community is made up of its own unique communities, from seminarians and ministerial candidates to members of the general public interested in matters of theology. Together, theological libraries can trial ideas, implement new services, and coordinate services to offer those that suit their local communities best.

Whilst there are similarities between theological libraries around the world, they are also quite different in many ways: different denominations, different clientele, different purchasing foci. Diversity brings innovation to organizations as well as to library associations (Smith 2016) through the presence and contributions of more nationalities, countries, and groups around the table. By focusing on a worldwide vision for theological libraries, Atla enables diverse voices to contribute in new and exciting ways.

Despite so much being achieved through the increased international focus of Atla, there is still much that can be done. How can we all contribute effectively to assist majority-world libraries in ways that may truly benefit them? Some collaborations, such as the Theological Libraries Ebook Lending Project (Campbell 2017), are currently only available to libraries in North America. Investigating how these resources can be accessed by theological libraries in all nations is an area for potential future development. Being able to share such resources amongst theological libraries throughout the world can distribute not only access to information but cost savings as well.

Budgetary and financial instability are major issues across almost all libraries. Exchange rates and conversion to local currency from USD and GBP can at times be unfavorable. Current ANZTLA consortial arrangements with major publishers such as SAGE, Oxford, and ESBCO, to name a few, have been extremely helpful. However, there are still a number of major players in the theology discipline that could be approached to offer reduced rates for members in a consortium. Atla's advocacy to publishers could be increased further afield for libraries outside North America. Another area that needs attention is communication and raising awareness of current trends. Greater organization and planning around communication strategies may help the global community of theological libraries increase its effectiveness. For example, there are opportunities to raise awareness of open source scholarly journals as freely available, tangible assets. A good and consistent communication plan that informs information professions, regardless of location, on such things as consortium pricing and free scholarly journals would make a significant impact.

Conclusion

ANZTLA and Atla are like-minded associations with similar histories and development pathways on opposite sides of the world, striving to achieve common outcomes and goals. Library cooperation and collaboration is far from dead in the theological library arena with our ongoing and growing relationship. Atla's collegiality is deeply valued by ANZTLA, and it is hoped that it will remain mutually beneficial long into the future. Atla's professionalism and strategic approach to move beyond the North American continent, as well as its relationship with and outreach to other theological associations such as the Association of British Theological and Philosophical Librarians (ABTAPL), the Bibliothèques

Européennes de Théologie (BETH), and the Forum of Asian Theological Librarians (ForATL), are also worthy of commendation.

Theological librarianship, no matter where the librarian may reside, is becoming more collaborative, more cooperative, and more communal. There are areas for potential further development, and if anything can be based on the growth of the continuing relationship between Atla and ANZTLA, it is that the future of theological librarianship everywhere is bright.

On the occasion of this special anniversary, ANZTLA is committed to continued collaboration with Atla in order to further our collective knowledge and expand our combined wisdom. We acknowledge and celebrate Atla's 75th anniversary with an eye to the future because, if we think of the possibilities offered by continued international collaboration, we can only see benefits to be shared by our patrons, staff, and researchers.

Works Cited

ANZTLA. 2015. *ATLA Strategic Plan*. www.atla.com/wp-content/uploads/2019/03/Atla-Strategic-Plan-2015.pdf.

——. 2007. "ANZTLA Constitution." *Australian and New Zealand Theological Library Association* 7. bit.ly/ANZTLAconstitution.

——. n.d. "Jeanette Little Scholarship Scheme." Accessed July 9, 2019. www.anztla.org/jeanette.

Atla. 2018. "International Theological Librarianship Education Task Force." *Atla.com*. www.atla.com/about/committees-councils-task-forces/itle-taskforce/.

Bailey-Hainer, Brenda. 2014. "Infinite Possibilities: The Future of Theological Librarianship." *ANZTLA EJournal* 13: 6–18. doi.org/10.31046/anztla.v0i13.511.

Ball, Les. "A Thematic History of Theological Education in Australia." In *Theological Education: Foundations, Practices, and Future Directions*, edited by Andrew M. Bain and Ian Hussey. Australian College of Theology Monograph Series. Wipf & Stock.

Bollier, John A. 2006. "Introduction." In *A Broadening Conversation: Classic Readings in Theological Librarianship*, edited by Melody Layton McMahon and David R. Stewart, 233–6. Lanham, MD: The Scarecrow Press. doi.org/10.31046/atlapress.27.

Burn, Kerrie. 2019. "Two Research and Publication Projects Related to Theological Libraries." *ANZTLA EJournal* 23: 120–1. doi.org/10.31046/anztla.v0i23.1667.

Campbell, Donna. 2017. "Theological Libraries Ebook Lending Project: Traditional and Revolutionary." *Atla Blog*, February 7, 2017.

www.atla.com/blog/theological-libraries-ebook-lending-project-traditional-and-revolutionary/.

Ćurić, Matina, ed. 2020. *The Theological Librarian's Handbook*. Chicago: Atla Open Press. *doi.org/10.31046/atlaopenpress.34*.

Edwards, Averill M. B. 1988. "Libraries and Librarians: An Undervalued Asset." *Australian and New Zealand Theological Library Association Newsletter* 6: 23. *doi.org/10.31046/anztla.v0i6.777*.

Elliott, L. R. 2006. "Six Years of ATLA: A Historical Sketch." In *A Broadening Conversation: Classic Readings in Theological Librarianship*, edited by Melody Layton McMahon and David R. Stewart, 240–8. Lanham, MD: The Scarecrow Press. *doi.org/10.31046/atlapress.27*.

Hall, Penelope R. 1997. "The International Council of Theological Library Associations: Past Foundation, Present Form and Plans for the Future." In *American Theological Library Association Summary of Proceedings* 51: 243–251.

Harmanny, Geert. 2016. "Some Reflections on Cooperation Between Theological Libraries and the Future of Theological Libraries in (and Outside) Europe." In *The Future of Theological Libraries in Indonesia (and South East Asia) and the Netherlands (and Europe)*, edited by Hélène Oosterdijk-Van Leeuwen and Wilijan Puttenstein, 22–5. Amsterdam: Protestant Theological University. *theoluniv.ub.rug.nl/60/*.

Harvey, Philip. 1989. "The Australasian Religion Index: A Progress Report." *ANZTLA Newsletter* 7: 18. *serials.atla.com/anztla/article/view/794/967*.

Hurd, Al. 1996. "Maximizing Theological Resources: The Role of New Technologies and the Internet for Theological Library Cooperation." *ANZTLA Newsletter* 28: 4–11. *doi.org/10.31046/anztla.v0i28.1003*.

Jones, Simon. 2019. "Ministerial Formation as Theological Education in the Context of Theological Study." *Journal of European Baptist Studies* 19, no. 1: 41–53. *doi.org/10.25782/jebs.v19i1.143*.

Kahl, Werner and Uta Andrée. 2017. "Ecumenical Formation in Theology (EcuFiT)." In *Theological Education and Theology of Life: Transformative Christian Leadership in the Twenty-First Century: A Festschrift for Dietrich Werner*, edited by Atola Longkumer, Huang Po Ho, and Uta Andrée, 252–60. London: Oxford Regnum Books International.

Lola, Cindy. 2019. "Atla-ANZTLA Scholarship Recipient Report." *ANZTLA EJournal* 23: 76–8. *doi.org/10.31046/anztla.v0i23.1664*.

McIntosh, Lawrence D., Philip Arthur Harvey, and Lynn Pryor, eds. 1995. *"So Great a Cloud of Witnesses": Libraries & Theologies: Festschrift in Honour of Lawrence D. McIntosh*. Melbourne: published jointly by the Uniting Church

Theological Hall and the Australian and New Zealand Theological Library Association. *doi.org/10.31046/atlapress.10*.

Millard, Ruth. 2010. "Better Together: Some Reflections on Library Cooperation and Consortia with Special Reference to ANZTLA Consortia." *ANZTLA EJournal* 15: 45–57. *doi.org/10.31046/anztla.vi5.203*.

Mintel, Richard H. 1990. "Current Developments in the American Theological Library Association." *ANZTLA Newsletter* 11: 9–13. *doi.org/10.31046/anztla.v0i11.827*.

O'Brien, Elmer J. 2006. "Building on Our Strengths for the Future." In *A Broadening Conversation: Classic Readings in Theological Librarianship,* edited by Melody Layton McMahon and David R. Stewart, 249–54. Lanham, MD: The Scarecrow Press. *doi.org/10.31046/atlapress.27*.

Olson, Ray A. 1997. "Memorial Tributes." *American Theological Library Association Summary of Proceedings* 51: 335–49.

Paull, Paula Kelly. n.d. "The Importance of Library Partnerships." *Princh Library Blog.* Accessed January 21, 2020. *bit.ly/Paull_Library_Parternships*.

Premadish, Nalini. 2018. "ATLA-ANZTLA Scholarship Recipient Report." *ANZTLA EJournal* 21: 49–52. *doi.org/10.31046/anztla.v0i11.827*.

"Report on ANZTLA Inaugural Conference." 1987. *ANZTLA EJournal* 1: 3–7. *doi.org/10.31046/anztla.v0i1.717*.

Robinson, Kim. 2010. "ANZTLA Keynote Address: 'ANZTLA, 25 Years: A Sterling Achievement'." *ANZTLA EJournal* 5: 25–33. *doi.org/10.31046/anztla.vi5.200*.

Smith, Bonnie J. 2016. "Broadening Our Scope: International Collaboration for Retooling the Academic Library." *Journal of Library Administration* 56: 395-415. *doi.org/10.1080/01930826.2016.1144929*.

Stanton, Maria. 2018. "It's a Wonderful Library!" *ANZTLA EJournal* 21: 6-15. *doi.org/10.31046/anztla.v0i21.945*.

Stevens, Kerrie, Siong Ng, Cindy Derrenbacker, and Kerrie Burn. 2020. "Australian and New Zealand Librarians Attend Atla Annual 2019." *ANZTLA EJournal* 24: 14-17. *doi.org/10.31046/anztla.v0i24.1814*.

Stuehrenberg, Paul F. 2009. "Theological Libraries and International Collaboration." Paper presented at the Forum of Asian Theological Librarians (ForATL) Conference, Trinity Theological College, Singapore, March 10–13, 2009. *www.foratl.org/papers/paulstuehrenberg.htm*.

White, Ernest G. 2006. "A Combined Greeting to ATLA 40 and Reflection on ATLA 1." In *A Broadening Conversation: Classic Readings in Theological Librarianship,* edited by Melody Layton McMahon and David R. Stewart, 264–8. Lanham, MD: The Scarecrow Press. *doi.org/10.31046/atlapress.27*.

Zweck, Trevor. 1985. "Theological Library Association Formed." *Colloquium* 18, no. 1: 71.

——. 1986. "Australian and New Zealand Theological Libraries and Librarianship." *American Theological Library Association Summary of Proceedings* 40: 88–100.

——. 1987. "American Theological Libraries and Librarianship: A View from Down Under." *ANZTLA Newsletter* 1: 8–15. doi.org/10.31046/anztla.v0i1.718.

——. 1993. "ANZTLA Affairs." *ANZTLA Newsletter* 19: 2–3. doi.org/10.31046/anztla.v0i19.907.

——. 1995. "A Decade of Working Together: The Establishment and Early History of the Australian and New Zealand Theological Library Association." In *"So Great a Cloud of Witnesses" : Libraries & Theologies : Festschrift in Honour of Lawrence D. McIntosh,* edited by Lawrence D. McIntosh, Philip Arthur Harvey, and Lynn Pryor, 13. Melbourne: published jointly by the Uniting Church Theological Hall and the Australian and New Zealand Theological Library Association. doi.org/10.31046/atlapress.10.

CHAPTER 8

A Threefold Cord

A Narrative and Reflection

CARISSE MICKEY BERRYHILL, ABILENE CHRISTIAN UNIVERSITY

Two are better than one, because they have a good reward for their toil. For if they fall, one will lift up the other; but woe to one who is alone and falls and does not have another to help. Again, if two lie together, they keep warm; but how can one keep warm alone? And though one might prevail against another, two will withstand one. A threefold cord is not quickly broken. (Ecclesiastes 4:9–12, NRSV)

O n the occasion of Atla's 75th anniversary, the preparation of this volume reminds me to be grateful for its 50th anniversary predecessor, which has been of so much use to my "Theological Librarianship" students and me. It is good both to look back and to look forward. Moreover, it is good to look back in order to look forward. What strengths of our profession indicate that we will successfully meet the challenges ahead? Let me answer that question with a story of how Atla helped me meet a professional challenge. After that look back, I will reflect on three key strengths it reveals about our profession.

I have been a member of Atla since 1992, when I began working as a librarian in an ATS-accredited seminary library. Until then, my professional formation had taken place exclusively in the context of the church of my childhood. Since I had grown up in a preacher's home and had attended and taught at colleges connected with my own religious upbringing, I did not know very many professional people outside my own church tradition.

That began to change when I came to know the folks of the Tennessee Theological Library Association (TTLA) and Atla. I will always remember the closing dinner of the 1994 Atla Annual conference in Pittsburgh, when we all sang together at the end of a dinner cruise, with Seth Kasten leading us, "Oh God, Our Help in Ages Past." The first woman I ever heard preach was Renita Weems at the 1995 Atla Annual hosted by Vanderbilt. The first time I was asked to lead prayer with men present was at the Wabash Colloquy for Theological Librarians in 2000.

The two most important papers that have shaped my professional life were read at Duke at Atla Annual 2001. Anne Womack's comment on her images of Chartres Cathedral still rings in my ears: "If you don't begin thinking now about making content digitally accessible, you will be standing on the curb when that bus pulls away." Herman Peterson's paper on the ministry of theological librarians as stewards, servants, and sages still helps me organize my teaching and speaking about our profession.

After twelve precious years in Tennessee, I moved to Texas in 2004. At the Atla Annual in Kansas City, a month after I started my new job, Executive Director Dennis Norlin recruited me to teach an online course in theological librarianship being jointly designed by Atla and the library program at University of Illinois Urbana-Champaign. Norlin soothed my protests with reassurances: the Atla Professional Development Committee had already prepared the syllabus and had nominated me. They knew I was an experienced professor and that I had been teaching online at my seminary in Tennessee. Illinois would handle the technological and administrative details. The course was scheduled to begin the fall of 2005, so I had a year to prepare. I checked with my dean and he checked with the provost, and then I agreed.

What followed the first excitement was a year of dread, with rising panic. I didn't have a PhD in library science. I had never taught library science at all, much less at Illinois. I had never managed a library. How could I teach librarianship when I had experience in only one area of library practice as a cataloger? How could I lecture two hours a week online about things I had never been responsible to do? What was I going to do with the 100-page syllabus that the Professional Development Committee had given me? How would I organize the content? What would I use for a textbook? I was choking, drowning, anticipating humiliation. I was sure I was alone and would fall, like the unfortunate person in the Ecclesiastes text: "Woe to one who is alone and falls and does not have another to help."

But desperation led to clarity. My pretended self-sufficiency broke down. I was not alone. I had others to help. I was part of a generous and hospitable community of practitioners, most of them with much more experience than I had in the subject I had been called to teach. For more than twelve years I had learned from my Atla colleagues first through my own library and the TTLA and then through Atla Annual. It finally occurred to me that my Atla colleagues, not I, had all that my students needed. It was just up to me to make the introductions.

Melody McMahon and David Stewart let me use the pre-print edition of *A Broadening Conversation* as a text. I began calling and emailing Atla folk to invite them to be interviewed about their experience in librarianship, in collection development, in teaching and reference and information literacy, in library management, preservation, exhibits, archives, serials, diversity, professional development. They said yes, and yes, and yes again. Now, fifteen years later, dozens of my Atla colleagues have answered the students' questions about purpose and practice. It has been a triumph of partnership and generosity for the sake of students. We have, as the text says, "a good reward for [our] toil."

It may be that, in this dreadful pandemic year of 2020, even while we look back at this moment in gratitude to celebrate our 75th anniversary, we might also be secretly besieged by paralyzing fears. Will we or our colleagues die? Will a global economic crisis destroy our academic institutions, our library budgets, our jobs? How will the economy affect our Atla products business? Will our Atla staff be able to continue to innovate? Even if we survive, how will new models of theological education emerge, accelerate, and change the way we carry out library work? How will our mission and identity be transformed by new global partnerships, interreligious dialogue, and developments in scholarly publishing and the information industry? Will our courage fail in the face of these challenges? We might, like the solitary ones in the Ecclesiastes text above, feel alone, and cold, and faced by foes.

Be of good courage. We have a three-fold cord of community.

We are not alone, because we are a community committed to stewardship of a body of knowledge both ancient and ever new, the human yearning to understand and experience the divine. We all are concerned with the vitality, quality, and accessibility of religious and theological studies worldwide. We understand that our efforts to preserve archival materials help our institutions interrogate and interpret their own history. We are busy expanding and diversifying scholarly work on our field of practice. We believe that libraries are the natural hub for institutions' development of platforms and best practices for scholarly communication. Like the laborers in Ecclesiastes, we work hard and carry a big load. But we know that if we stagger or fall, someone in our community will help us solve the problems, pick us up, help us learn, or lead us to think in new ways. We have deep reservoirs of subject domain knowledge, a real sense of the direction that academic scholarship in religion is going and where it is yet lacking. Our everyday purpose of identifying religious knowledge to collect for preservation is the first cord that binds us together.

We are warm instead of shivering alone because we are a community committed to a professional culture of service—a set of habits, skills, and values that have forged our identity. Whether we are concerned with acquisition, preservation, arrangement and description, access, assistance, or the technological innovations that are transforming each of these, we know and discuss and develop and support good practices. We also cherish values that give our practices meaning, such as access to information, freedom of inquiry, the right of researchers to own their own voices, civil and religious liberty, hospitality to diverse voices. We may be excruciatingly helpful, but we are also fiercely intellectual. We believe in knowing and being known. Our subject material is infused with awe that humbles us and challenges our character. We value the dignity of inquiry as an act of faith. We possess that central conviction of humane education: knowledge of the truth frees. The millions of details of text and bibliography and source code that pass through our hands form a vast web of connection between the voices of the past and the students and faculty and pastors and scholars whom we serve. Our professional culture of connecting people with resources welcomes and empowers and releases creativity. Our profession of service is the second cord that binds us together.

We are wise in withstanding forces that threaten our professional mission because we are a community committed to relationships in teaching and learning. First, in our own institutional settings we have valuable partnerships with our colleagues, the faculties, the administrative officers, and the accrediting associations whose standards we voluntarily develop and agree to. Furthermore, we as members exercise moral ownership of our own professional association, including its bylaws, its endowment, and the policies by which our elected board governs Atla's business operations. We express our imagination of the good through Atla's institutional ends. Most importantly, we have a robust relational infrastructure of cooperation and conversation among ourselves. Whether in regional meetings, Atla Annual, or in the work of committees and interest groups, we know and respect and stand with one another. We worship together. We remember those we have lost. We welcome the newcomers. We tackle big problems by working together. Sometimes we quibble. But because we understand hospitality—that ability to restrain one's own point of view sufficiently to learn from others—we develop trust. Our wisdom as teachers and learners in community is the third cord that binds us together.

We do not know what lies ahead. We don't know how we will solve the problems that will arise. Will seminaries close or merge? Probably. Will the economy of libraries change? Probably. Will we still be a community? Certainly. We have, in a way, been preparing for a long time to meet the crisis. When I felt absolutely terrified fifteen years ago, Atla had already been at work for six decades building collections, expertise, and relationships–the very things I needed to meet my own little challenge when I finally admitted that I couldn't succeed alone. If anyone in theological education can figure out how to go forward, we will do that because we will do it together. We have been at work for 75 years, bound together by our purpose and our professionalism and our relationships with one another. Theological librarians will serve and succeed because we rely on one another. We are bound together by stewardship, service, and wisdom. A threefold cord is not easily broken.

Contributors

Carisse Mickey Berryhill is special collections librarian at Abilene Christian University's Brown Library. She served on the Atla Board from 2006 to 2012 and was appointed to the International Theological Librarianship Education Task Force in 2018. Since 2005, she has taught an Atla-sponsored course on Theological Librarianship at the University of Illinois. She holds a PhD in English from Florida State University.

Matthew S. Collins is currently the library director at Alma College, in Alma, Michigan. He served as the library director at Louisville Presbyterian Theological Seminary and as a reference librarian at the Pitts Theology Library at Candler School of Theology at Emory University. He has a PhD in New Testament from Vanderbilt University and a an MLIS from Florida State University. His primary research interests are the Gospel of Luke and information literacy in undergraduate students.

Stephen D. Crocco has been the director of the Yale Divinity Library since 2015. Prior to Yale, he was the James Lenox Librarian at Princeton Theological Seminary and, before that, the library director at Pittsburgh Theological Seminary. He has a PhD in religious ethics from Princeton University and an MLS from the University of Pittsburgh.

James Estes is a supervisory librarian at the Library of Congress, after having served as theology librarian and director of the library at Wesley Theological Seminary. In addition to his federal service, he is an editor for Books@Atla Open

Press, and maintains professional research interests in book history, information literacy, and scholarly communications. As a medievalist and church historian, he studies, teaches, and writes about the history of Christian spirituality, focusing on medieval English vernacular theology. He holds an MSLS from the Catholic University of America, where he also received his PhD in theology and religious studies.

Shawn Goodwin works as the metadata control analyst at Atla. His research interests include digital humanities, ancient Near Eastern languages and cultures, and the Hebrew Bible. His GitHub profile can be found at *e2dubba.github.io*.

Andrew Keck currently serves as executive director of strategic initiatives and special assistant to the dean at Perkins School of Theology at Southern Methodist University. Before a career pivot, he served for six years as library director of Luther Seminary and thirteen years on the staff of the library of Duke Divinity School. He earned his theological degree and served as a student worker in the library of Boston University School of Theology. While earning his library science degree at Clarion University of Pennsylvania, he worked paraprofessionally in the library of Pittsburgh Theological Seminary and at the Bertelsmann Music Group Archives.

Evan Kuehn is assistant professor of information literacy at Brandel Library, North Park University. His books include *Troeltsch's Eschatological Absolute* (Oxford University Press, 2020) and *Theology Compromised: Schleiermacher, Troeltsch, and the Possibility of a Sociological Theology* (co-authored with Matthew Ryan Robinson, Lexington/Fortress Press, 2019). His main research interests are 19th–20th century Protestant thought, information literacy and research methods, and qualitative and empirical methods in theological research.

Siong Ng is the library manager at Carey Baptist College in Auckland, New Zealand. She was president of the Australia and New Zealand Theological Library Association (ANZTLA) from 2015–18. She has presented papers at various conferences, including twice at Atla Annual, and has written a number of journal articles. Siong holds a bachelor's degree in music and a master's degree in information and library studies and music.

Alexander Luis Odicino is an MLIS degree candidate at the University of Denver and an Ask a Librarian apprentice with the University of Colorado Boulder University Libraries.

Christopher A. Rogers is director of the library at Mundelein Seminary/University of Saint Mary of the Lake, where he is also on the academic faculty teaching courses in theological literacy, research, and writing and history of Christianity. He previously taught for ten years at DePaul University in history and religious studies. He is currently engaged in a collaborative project with select Midwestern colleges and universities to digitize for scholarly access USML's medieval-era manuscripts as well as a similar joint effort with the Gregorian University in Rome. He has written several journal articles and given conference talks on topics in early modern Christian history. He received a PhD in religious history from Northwestern University, MDiv in theology from Southern Methodist University, and MLIS from the University of Texas at Austin in archives and special collections.

Myka Kennedy Stephens is seminary librarian and associate professor of theological bibliography at Lancaster Theological Seminary in Lancaster, PA. She serves as an editor for Books@Atla Open Press and is actively involved in the Southeastern Pennsylvania Theological Library Association and the Koha open source ILS community. She regularly writes and presents on strategic and integrated planning for libraries, open source solutions for libraries, and the future of small theological libraries. She holds a Master of Divinity degree from Emory University and a Master of Science in Library and Information Studies degree from Florida State University.

Kerrie Stevens, AALIA(CP), MAppSci(LibMgt), BBus(Info&LibMgt), is the director of library services at Alphacrucis College–the national training college of the Australian Christian Churches, with six Australian campus libraries servicing students from vocational to doctoral level. As a long-time position holder (president, vice-president, secretary, statistician, *ANZTLA EJournal* manager) within the Australian and New Zealand Theological Library Association (ANZTLA), Kerrie has almost two decades of interaction and experience with theological libraries across Australia and New Zealand.

Paul A. Tippey is the dean of library and information technology services as well as a faculty member within the Beeson School of Practical Theology at Asbury Theological Seminary, where he has been employed since 2001. Dr. Tippey holds a PhD in organization leadership from Regent University in addition to two master's degrees–in library and information sciences from the University of Illinois and in theology from Asbury Theological Seminary. In his free time, Dr. Tippey enjoys construction projects, working on his homestead, and spending time with his wife and children.

Megan E. Welsh is the interdisciplinary arts & humanities librarian and an associate professor at the University of Colorado (CU) Boulder in Boulder, CO. She has been the subject specialist for religious studies, Jewish studies, and classics since joining CU Boulder in fall 2013. Additionally, Megan actively engages in Atla committee and interest group work and has presented several times at Atla Annual. Her current research interests include studying the intersection between personally held religious beliefs and professional library practice, and academic libraries as centers of community and dialogic practices.

Made in the USA
Las Vegas, NV
26 January 2021

16288099R00090